Pursuit *of* Happiness

An Introduction to the Libertarian Ethos of
Charles Erskine Scott Wood

Alan L. Contreras

Liberty means the right to peaceably say all things and peaceably do
all things; being answerable for the consequences.

C.E.S. Wood

2014

Much of C.E.S. Wood's work, including *Imperialism vs. Democracy, On Privilege, Transmutation of Virtues into Vices* and the 1902 Manhattan Club address is in the public domain. Permission for use of material from *Too Much Government* has been granted by the Wood family.

Pursuit of Happiness: An Introduction to the Libertarian Ethos of Charles Erskine Scott Wood.

ISBN-13: 978-1502907097
ISBN-10: 1502907097

Pursuit *of* Happiness

An Introduction to the Libertarian Ethos of
Charles Erskine Scott Wood

Alan L. Contreras

By Alan Contreras

Education

College and State: Resources and Philosophies
The Mind on Edge: An Introduction to John Jay Chapman's Philosophy of Higher Education

Essays/Letters/Other Nonfiction

Pursuit of Happiness: An Introduction to the Libertarian Ethos of C.E.S. Wood
Concerto in Q: Essays, Reviews and Travels 1982-2013
Song After All: The Letters of Reginald Shepherd and Alan Contreras
Afield: Forty Years of Birding the American West

Poetry

Firewand
Night Crossing
Fieldwork (chapbook)

Ornithology

Handbook of Oregon Birds (with Hendrik Herlyn)
Birds of Lane County, Oregon (editor)
Birds of Oregon: a General Reference (with D. B. Marshall and M. G. Hunter)
Northwest Birds in Winter

Dedicated to my friend

Graham Floyd

fellow Oregonian, fellow birder,
man of honor, lover of truth, champion of freedom

Contents

❖ Introduction ❖

Charles Erskine Scott Wood (1852-1944) is a symbol of western individualism and was at one time one of the nation's best-known advocates for human freedom. That he is rarely remembered today says more about our cultural habit of forgetfulness and moving on than it does about his own virtues and impact on society. This introductory publication about Wood's individualist philosophy is intended to provide the reader with enough interest to support a more complete reading of Wood's work.[1] Material that is otherwise no longer easily available, some of which is Wood's clearest work about his philosophy, is reprinted here.

There are several good biographical sources for information on Wood's life. Among these are the excellent collection *Wood Works* (Edwin Bingham and Tim Barnes, cited herein as *WW*), an anthology of his writings with useful biographical notes; *Two Rooms: A Life of Charles Erskine Scott Wood,* a well-executed traditional biography by Robert Hamburger; the warm and colloquial *Life of Charles Erskine Scott Wood* by his son Erskine Wood and George Venn's *Soldier to Advocate: C.E.S. Wood's 1877 Legacy,* which nominally covers Wood's time in Alaska and the Nez Perce conflict in which the young Wood served as an Army officer but in fact provides a wider look at Wood as an artist. It also offers a unique narrative of how the Wood family and Nez

---

[1] His work was extraordinarily varied, including poetry, dramatic works, speeches, fiction, essays and even songs. Excerpts from a sample of these can be found in *Wood Works*.

Perce Chief Joseph's family have remained connected over the years.

All of these discuss to some extent Wood's advocacy for individual freedom and are therefore essential reading for anyone interested in the subject, but none attempt to corral the varied and sometimes conflicting libertarian tendencies of Wood's life into a coherent picture of that philosophy. One reason for this is that Wood's views changed over time. One commentator noted that "[b]efore he had much to rebel against, the seeds of an ostentatious defiance against authority were already within him."[2] Another pointed out that during Wood's time at West Point he more than once "accumulated demerits just short of the number that would bring dismissal," [3] which suggests that his strong individualism affected his comfort with Army discipline.

Wood's life sometimes contained contradictions that tended to short-circuit any straightforward analysis of what, in fact, his philosophy was. For example, he was both a corporate lawyer and an advocate for the elimination of the privileges of wealth – at least some of them. See the reprint *On Privilege* included here for a discussion of this contrast by Wood himself, in the guise of a discussion among others.

This book attempts to sort Wood's multifaceted ideas into an orderly array, recognizing that this is a first step and

---

[2] I do not know this commentator's full name, but her writing about Wood and the free love movement is quite good and she appeared for several years as the "Polywog" blog; see http://polywog.wordpress.com/luisa-capetillo-and-charles-erskine-scott-wood-free-love-and-the-state-at-the-turn-of-the-twentieth-century/

[3] Edwin R. Bingham, "Oregon's Romantic Rebels: John Reed and Charles Erskine Scott Wood." *Pacific Northwest Quarterly* 50(3): 77, 78 (1959).

that other scholars may want to review even more of Wood's work, such as his letters and his less accessible published work.

The word "libertarian" as used in the title is a translation of Wood's frequent claims to be an anarchist. Although the term "anarchist" was much in the news especially in the latter half of Wood's life, what it really meant at the time was a rather wide mixture comprising the outer edges of labor organizing, some variants of socialism, destructive impulses against American institutions and what we would today recognize as libertarianism.

Wood remains underappreciated in American history and the kind of individualism that Wood espoused remains a significant part of the social culture of the western United States, in particular, and increasingly of a large minority of American voters. Western historian Edwin Bingham wrote of Wood that

> "[i]n almost everything he wrote he implied or decried the unfairness of the prevailing economic and political system, urging the minimalization of government and removal of inhibitions on social and individual freedoms. In short, he was much closer to Henry George or Emma Goldman than to Hiram Johnson or Teddy Roosevelt."[4]

Bingham also rightly pointed out that Wood's "revolt is difficult to define," noting that the nature of the rebellion changed from a highly personal, over-the-top dandyism in his

---

[4] Edwin R. Bingham, *Charles Erskine Scott Wood*, Western Writers Series No. 94, Boise State University, 1990, p. 23.

Army years and early professional life to a "more humanitarian" independence by 1918.[5]

Wood was responsible[6] for the iconic version of Chief Joseph's "I will fight no more forever" speech that has come down to us as western gospel. He was also in part responsible  for distributing his friend Mark Twain's notorious pamphlet "1601," a colorful, elaborated conversation on the farting habits of Queen Elizabeth I's court. This gives us a starting point for appreciation of the breadth of his capacity and enthusiasms.

Add to that his ideas about what would come to be called free love, his position as a prominent Portland corporate lawyer and informal arbiter of regional artistic norms, his spectacular defenses of anarchist Emma Goldman and the right of Filipinos to self-determination, and his hilarious collection of satirical God-chat *Heavenly Discourse*, and we know more.

---

[5] Edwin R. Bingham, "Oregon's Romantic Rebels: John Reed and Charles Erskine Scott Wood." *Pacific Northwest Quarterly* 50(3): 77, 88-89 (1959).

[6] Most commentators seem confident that Wood assembled the final version of this "speech" from several things that Joseph said during the period of surrender, and that it is something more than a translation, bearing Wood's own distinctive tone. However, the speech was clearly based on things Joseph actually said, unlike the completely bogus "Chief Seattle" quotes that appear in many venues. The "translation" is discussed in more detail in the biographies. The character of Wood was played by Sam Elliott in the 1975 movie *I Will Fight No More Forever*.

Somewhere at the intersection of his concerns with free love and personal liberty on the one hand and political freedoms on the other comes his support for various radical causes and their advocates. In his professional life he was an active defender of Margaret Sanger's efforts to advance family planning at a time when this was considered offensive or even illegal. He also defended Dr. Marie Equi,[7] a curious character whose lesbian arrangements involved several women and whose political radicalism and erratic behavior eventually resulted in her imprisonment for helping Sanger distribute birth-control literature in Portland, although apparently Equi's use of a bullwhip on a male civic leader in another community did not rise to criminal charges. Wood's defense of Equi in an appellate brief, well worth reading, is reprinted in part in *Wood Works*.

His inconsistent gifts as a poet resulted in some overwrought and preachy work, loaded to the ground with baroque phrasing. It also produced some exceptional passages on the desert, human imperfection and the more refined aspects of love, sometimes cohabiting the same poem as the more labored sections. His painting and drawing, almost unknown today, is equal to that of anyone else in its depiction of the American west. A portion of that art is available at the Huntington Museum and some is available online.

Tim Barnes, George Venn and Chris Weiss reviewed the manuscript and their comments were of considerable value. Professor Mary Wood at the University of Oregon law school was kind enough to look at the manuscript and lend her

---

[7] A biography of Dr. Equi is scheduled to appear from Oregon State University Press in 2015.

enthusiasm to this book about her great-grandfather. Thanks to E.J. Carter from Special Collections at the Lewis and Clark College Archives for assistance with the cover photo of Wood. Finally, thanks to Nathan Williams for his invaluable assistance with proofreading the text, a tedious task that saved the author many embarrassments. I am, of course, responsible for any errors that remain.

Alan Contreras
Eugene, Oregon
November, 2014

An Introduction to the Libertarian Ethos
of Charles Erskine Scott Wood

❖ C.E.S. Wood's Themes of Freedom ❖

The word "multifaceted" is uniquely applicable to Wood's ideas because he seemed to be facing rather firmly in several directions at the same time. This man who lived grandly (and wanted to live even more grandly) and strode easily in the upper balconies of Portland, San Francisco and New York society was the same man who preached anarchy, followed his sexual desires wherever they went, represented the bankers Lazard Freres in major land deals but loathed the unearned privileges of wealth, socialized naturally with writers Lincoln Steffens and Mark Twain, and worked primarily as a corporate lawyer. His combination of political libertarianism and an appreciation for the nicer things in life is reminiscent of the life of his near-contemporary: the writer, editor and social theorist Albert Jay Nock (1870-1945).

Wood had grave doubts about the more violent and destructive aspects of the assemblage of activities called anarchism and indeed refused to represent the *Los Angeles Times* bombers, leading to their representation by Clarence Darrow in one of his sleazier moments.[8]

If we are to seek a definitive statement of Wood's individualist philosophy, we can look in almost any direction. Not only was he a man of varied interests, he was comfortable in front of many audiences. Few speakers would have felt

---

[8] For more detail on how Darrow got involved in the case and how nasty it was, see ch. 22 in *Two Rooms*, in which the tale of bribery, backroom dealings and other gutter tactics are discussed. Hamburger notes that "As Wood foresaw, Darrow did his best to circumvent the law."

perfectly at home, as Wood did, saying to the Manhattan Club that

> I come from the west, where in a civilization founded on the mine and the camp, we believe that the saloon and the theater has as good a right to be open on Sunday as the church and the school. I come from where we think that it is the right of every American to go to hell and be damned if he wants to. That is not humor—it is the truth.[9]

This in-your-face naturalism is reminiscent of such situations as Benjamin Franklin parading his unadorned person in France in the early 1780s, Walt Whitman sharing his colorful yawp with the world or John Jay Chapman denouncing politics to a room full of politicians.[10] It represents a certain identifiable strain of American vigor and independence.

Wood's commitment to this independence was not simply a public face. He inscribed a gift of the meditations of Marcus Aurelius to his son Erskine thus:

> The sum of wisdom is to avoid dogmatism and tyranny—to always keep in mind that you yourself may be wrong—and to leave each to live his own life unburdened by even

---

[9] From Wood's speech to Democrats at the Manhattan Club on Feb. 22, 1902, as quoted by Bingham and Barnes in *Wood Works: the Life and Writings of Charles Erskine Scott Wood*, Oregon State U. Press, 1997. Additional excerpts from this speech appear herein.

[10] Chapman frequently criticized the civic leaders of New England and the nation in his writings and speeches. His later years were quieter than Wood's and, in Chapman's case, much less visible as he fired occasional missives from the comforts of his New York estate. See Richard Hovey, *John Jay Chapman: Am American Mind* (Columbia 1959) and other works on Chapman for examples, many of which are also reprinted in the *Collected Works of John Jay Chapman* (Bernstein 1970).

> advice tyrannously insisted on—freedom to develop upward
> means necessarily freedom to develop downward—it is
> better some should go down than that this great law of
> freedom should be violated.[11]

Thus his commitment to freedom was buttressed by an understanding of consequences and an appreciation of the realities of daily life. This is apparent in the main themes of his personalized libertarian philosophy. These are divided into Political Freedoms, Social Freedoms and Commercial Freedoms for convenience in discussion, although they are in some ways more seamless than such a division would admit, and each broad category contains distinctive subunits.

The Libertarian Framework

The literature of Libertarianism (with a reasonably upper-case "L") is substantial, although until recent years much of it was either indigestible to a general reader (Austrian economists such as Friedrich Hayek and their American followers) or existed in the form of fiction (Ayn Rand and, to a lesser extent, science fiction writers such as Robert Heinlein). The widening interest in Libertarianism among the public, including young people, has resulted in the publication of several recent books that a reader interested in the subject might profitably ingest.

---

[11] This book inscription was reported by Erskine Wood in his *Life of Charles Erskine Scott Wood*, 1978 (1991), Rose Wind Press. For its origin in C.E.S. Wood's early life, see the story set forth on page 170.

The lion in this jungle is Brian Doherty's *Radicals for Capitalism: a freewheeling history of the modern American libertarian movement* (Public Affairs, 2007). At 619 pages, plus almost 100 pages of notes, just looking at it could cause any potential reader to wilt; it is not a fast or simple read, but it is no drudgery either, and provides a remarkably detailed history of how what we know today as American libertarianism came to exist. It is, in effect, a one-volume encyclopedia on the subject, and the fact that it does not mention C.E.S. Wood at all suggested a need for the present volume.

For someone interested in the subject but whose time and energy is somewhat more limited, David Boaz's *Libertarianism: a Primer* (Free Press, 1997) is an excellent way to get a functional knowledge of the history and especially the modern political activity of libertarianism without drowning in detail. For a more prescriptive look at how libertarian philosophy might be applied to particular modern social and political issues, Nick Gillespie and Matt Welch recently offered *The Declaration of Independents: how Libertarian Politics can Fix What's Wrong with America* (Public Affairs, 2011).

C.E.S. Wood is a legitimate part of the history of American libertarian thought, particularly in the West. He wrote on many themes of importance to personal freedom before such ideas were thought "respectable," he spoke on these issues before prestigious audiences where less reputable rabble-rousers could not go, and, not without significance to the permeation of such ideas into the mainstream, both his writing and his speaking abilities were greatly superior to those of many others who might have advanced the same ideas.

❖ Political Freedoms ❖

We are accustomed today to think of the Republican party as being oriented toward economic and certain kinds of individual freedoms, if not of social liberalism. However, in the late 1800s, the parties were situated differently, and Wood was associated with what became known as the "Mugwump" branch of the Democratic party, which emerged in the 1880s. He was eventually involved in the "New Democratic Party" (NDP) that nominated a highly qualified but spectacularly geriatric[12] presidential slate in 1896, splitting the vote with William Jennings Bryan and resulting in Republican William McKinley winning.

These Democrats, which might be known as "economic freedom" Democrats, rallied around individual rights. One writer noted of the NDP that

> "[f]or more than a century, it declared, the Democrats had believed "in the ability of every individual, unassisted, if unfettered by law, to achieve his own happiness" and had upheld his "right and opportunity peaceably to pursue whatever course of conduct he would, provided such conduct deprived no other individual of the equal enjoyment of the same right and opportunity." They had stood for "freedom of speech, freedom of conscience, freedom of trade, and freedom of contract, all of which are

---

[12] Sen. John C. Palmer of Illinois was 79 and his running mate, Kentucky Gov. Simon Bolivar Buckner, was 73.

implied by the century-old battle-cry of the Democratic Party, 'Individual Liberty'."[13]

This combines a somewhat raw economic freedom with a kind of civil liberties absolutism, which is essentially a statement of Wood's outlook, as well as a precursor of what we would call the libertarian philosophy today: economic freedom and a hands-off approach to social issues and international involvements. However, Wood was more concerned about the poor than are many modern-day libertarians. For an illuminating insight into how he thought about the problem of economic inequality, see the three-part "conversation" bearing the title of convenience "On Privilege" reprinted herein. See also the Manhattan Club Speech, which includes some extremely frank comments directed at the urban elite Democrats of the northeastern United States.

Leaders involved in the NDP remained active in politics and society, but

"few dared to go as far as C. E. S. Wood. As a lawyer, he not only represented dissidents such as Emma Goldman but crossed the line into anarchism. After the turn of the century, he wrote articles for anarchist and other radical journals, such as *Liberty*, *The Masses*, and *Mother Earth*. Until his death in 1944, Wood advocated such

---

[13] David T. Beito and Linda Royster Beito, "Gold Democrats and the Decline of Classical Liberalism 1896-1900." *The Independent Review* IV(4) Spring 2000, pp. 555-575. The Beito article notes that Wood actually served as a leader of this group, which was otherwise largely northeastern: "the most colorful member of the national committee was Charles Erskine Scott Wood of Oregon, a lawyer, essayist, poet, friend of Mark Twain, and graduate of West Point." ibid, p. 560.

unfashionable causes as free love, birth control, and anti-imperialism."[14]

In *Wood Works*, the authors note that Wood's reading included "Jefferson, Thoreau, Marx, the French anarchist Proudhon, the Russian anarchist Kropotkin, and single-taxer Henry George."[15] This was an underpinning for what he called philosophical anarchism, a close match with what we would call libertarianism today.

Equality of Liberty: Wood as Anarchist or Libertarian?

Was Wood really an anarchist? That depends on how we choose to define the term. His own writings on the subject are widely varied. One of his *Pacific Monthly* articles (reprinted in *Wood Works* p. 107) makes clear his commitment to individual freedom and free speech accomplished without violence. In that article, a good introduction to his views, he notes that "[t]yranny depends upon power, not upon the form of government; it exists in a republic where the power is secured by a majority, as well as in a kingdom, where it is "God-given."

Wood did not want a society completely free of social structures or even completely free of appropriate governance, he wanted as much individual freedom as possible consistent

---

[14] Beito, p. 570, citing Hamburger (1998).
[15] WW, p. 16.

with *civilization*.[16] For that reason he had no problem working within the structures of civilization while trying to improve them. In this he is aligned more closely with the future wing of libertarianism associated with Milton Friedman—a practical, functional, "good government" approach—than with some of the more radical branches that suppose a hypothetical, perfectible social universe free from disruptive currents.

In his desire to improve the way we govern ourselves, he opposed violence, at least after his time in the Army, thus:

> In all instances, Erskine argued that his anarchism was nonviolent, insisting that the fundamental doctrine of anarchism holds that in all matters there shall be the greatest amount of individual liberty compatible with equality of liberty. In 1912, a writer in *Sunset* put a favorable, even a conservative, spin on Wood's anarchism when he wrote that Wood "would like to see larger experiments in freedom, because freedom gives the widest scope to self-interest, and self-interest is the primal governing force."[17]

On the basic idea of liberty, particularly in a political sense, Wood noted in a discussion of other anarchists and how they were treated:

---

[16] Wood's original title for *Poet in the Desert* was *Civilization*, perhaps indicative of the centrality of the idea to his thinking. I am indebted to Tim Barnes for pointing this out.

[17] WW, page 106. Of some note is that Wood consistently promoted the utility of selfishness, thus becoming a distant precursor of Ayn Rand. His notion of the role of selfishness was more balanced and constrained than hers, and assumed that it could fit within—indeed, was necessary to—civilized society as he knew it.

Have we got to learn all over again what the world is supposed to have learned hundreds of years ago, that the greatest safety lies in liberty and the greatest danger in tyrannous repression? You can not imprison ideas. You can not kill them. There is one thing certain, that the progress of humanity has been toward liberty, and there is another thing certain, that humanity will still continue to progress toward liberty, and those who would gain for the world more liberty are true prophets, and those who would take away anything of the liberty which has been so dearly gained are walking backward into a pit.[18]

Wood was not an anarchist in the sense that we would use the term today. He was not really an anarchist even in the sense that the word was used in the early 20th Century. Even Emma Goldman referred to him as "a libertarian in the truest sense" in her 1931 autobiography.[19] When she came to Portland in 1908 to espouse radical causes, he enabled her to find a venue after her original contracts were cancelled, and also introduced her in a speech that apparently made her seem more lamb than lion – of course she roared all the same. This event is curiously similar to the actions of Eleanor Roosevelt arranging for Marian Anderson to sing at the

---

[18] From *Pacific Monthly* (1904), reprinted in *WW*, p. 112.

[19] Anarchist Emma Goldman (1869-1940), born in modern-day Lithuania but an American since her late teens, traveled the country speaking on subjects such as labor rights, birth control and prison reform. She was often the flashpoint for clamorous events. Her appearance in Portland in 1908 caused considerable ruckus. For details about this event, see *Two Rooms* p. 143 et seq.

Lincoln memorial after the Daughters of the American Revolution denied her the use of Constitution Hall.

His philosophy was in fact closer to modern libertarianism—a doctrine that allows for the greatest individual freedom consistent with people's duty not to harm others. This is essentially what the epigraph taken from *Too Much Government* says: "Liberty means the right to peaceably say all things and peaceably do all things; being answerable for the consequences."

Wood rarely reacted strongly against the customary everyday functions of government (in common with Albert Jay Nock, he distinguished the idea of government from the idea of the state). He mounted his soapbox mainly in response to government intrusion into the private sphere, which in his view was a substantial sphere indeed, yet not all-inclusive.

He was essentially a free-speech absolutist; his defenses of Emma Goldman were in that category and his general attitude was similar to that of his near-contemporary John Jay Chapman, who famously said that people should be given "raw truth – they think they will die" when they hear it, yet hear it they must.[20]

Wood supported *equality of liberty*: the idea that each person should be free to pursue life as she or he saw fit, subject only to the necessary protection of other people. To him, equality of liberty included the idea that those in positions of power or privilege did not have the right to stand in the way of, or oppress, those with whom they disagreed. In his view, this was true whether the oppressor was the government or the wealthy, but he had particular scorn for

---

[20] This quotation is from "Between Elections," from *Practical Agitation*, p. 49. Included in *Collected Works of John Jay Chapman* Vol 2.

government bureaucrats and their associated thugs who acted to oppress those with whom they disagreed. This was the theme of *Too Much Government*, which focused on Prohibition, and could be found in many other works as well. It is perhaps most clearly set forth in some of the text reprinted herein as "On Privilege," an example of which follows.

> **Demos**: This is what I say: that the field of struggle is not free and equal to all; that the mother earth, source of all wealth, is given by Special Privilege to a few; that society in general is taxed for a few; that the great economic forces and engines of society are monopolized by a few. And these Special Privileges, like so many conduit pipes, carry the wealth created by the many into the hands of the few beneficiaries of privilege.

Wood perceived the State as a captive of *privileged* people,[21] therefore his libertarianism was not limited to economic freedom as is that of some writers. One of his ideals was that in escaping the grasping claw of the State, a free person also should by so doing escape domination by the wealthy and powerful. This bears a certain similarity to Nock's outlook, which supposed a freedom in which justice had meaning *and* no one should have to pay for it:

> The state's whole duty is, first, to abstain entirely from any positive regulation of the individual's conduct; and,

---

[21] In a nutshell, Wood thought that "privilege is an advantage which is not a right" as set forth in the dialogue on privileges.

second, to make justice easily and costlessly accessible to every applicant.[22]

This combination of requirements: freedom of personal action and freedom from injustice imposed by external power, is also a key factor in Wood's philosophy.

The United States in the World

Wood focused his oratorical energy and his writing on domestic policy, free speech and issues of the American West. He made few extensive excursions into international policy. One of Wood's more remarkable and less known commentaries was his speech about the way the United States treated the people of the Philippines during and after the Spanish-American war. The speech, entitled "Imperialism vs. Democracy," was an address at the Jefferson Birthday Dinner, an event in Portland, Oregon on April 13, 1899. It was originally published[23] in *Pacific Monthly* and is reprinted in its entirety in this volume.

The essence of Wood's concern stated in this spectacular speech (worthy of much greater modern recognition) is this. The U.S. supported freedom for the people of Cuba because it suited us to do so, while we declined to apply the same standard to the people of the Philippines, over whom we chose to exercise what we called a protectorate and Wood considered little more than imperialist thuggery. At the end of

---

[22] Albert Jay Nock, *The Disadvantages of Being Educated*, p. 31. Hallberg (1996).
[23] C.E.S. Wood, "Imperialism vs. Democracy," *Pacific Monthly*, Vol II, May 1899-October 1899, p. 55-67.

the speech he encouraged the Filipinos to fight against the United States and kick us out, an unusual position to take in a speech at an American political event in a time of nationalist fervor.

❖ Economic Freedoms ❖

If Wood supported equality of liberty, what does that mean for his place in the list of libertarian thinkers? He was something of a classical liberal in the mold of Albert Jay Nock, but Nock was so steeped in the classical tradition that he was somewhat circumscribed by his own commitment to the literary past and perhaps to related notions of propriety. Wood was more a creature of the broad-shouldered West, arguing for a man's right to go straight to hell if he chose, with a quick stop at the saloon on Sunday for some fortification. It is hard to imagine Nock in such a bracing atmosphere, stuffing a copy of Cicero into the same leather satchel as the booze. It is not at all difficult to envision Wood doing that very thing.

The answer really depends on what libertarianism is conceived to be. At times, the idea of libertarianism seems to be little more than a cramped grasping for money, its symbol a clawing hand gripping a rotted abacus, rising above a sea of proles. To the extent that the politically visible arm of this philosophy limits itself to such a narrow economic possessiveness, it will remain a fringe movement, at base not very interesting outside professional economic circles: a theory that will never be a practice, so no one cares. Yet because of the way western societies work, economic freedoms are at the core of much useful thought about making society better. In effect, libertarian thinking requires that other economic philosophies explain themselves better.

Much of the visibility of libertarianism has been because of the economic views of its leaders (to the extent that it has leaders) and the economists who have carried its water. Wood comes from another angle. His interest in economic freedom is secondary to his interest in social and political freedom, yet he does have an interest in all of these, particularly land and property issues. He had a westerner's view of the land that tended to favor users over owners. At the same time, he had no time for the exercise of authority by those who occupied positions of privilege and, in his view, misused or wasted those positions to the detriment of society. His outlook was a subspecies of *noblesse oblige* perhaps unique to the American West.

Wood's own domestic economy appears to have been remarkably ephemeral at some points in his life, when he apparently lived well owing to the courtesy of his creditors rather to any great flow of income. He viewed wealth earned by the sweat of someone's brow as far more respectable than inherited swag or wealth gained by charging rents or otherwise benefitting from other people's work. This differential view of the sources of wealth carried over into his view of land ownership, apparent in almost all of his writings on the subject.

The idea that a privilege, including economic privilege, should be earned, and that it carried with it certain expectations of cultural citizenship, placed Wood a lot closer to libertarian thinkers such as Nock and Robert Nozick than it did to Hayek or other "absolutist" libertarian thinkers. Wood perceived an obligation to community that many libertarians do not, and he was more interested in practice than in theory.

There are certain similarities between Wood's outlook and that of John Jay Chapman, though Chapman circulated almost exclusively in the privileged parts of New England society, as they both placed a high value on truth versus money - on paper. Thus they disliked the ability of those with certain social privileges rooted in wealth to obscure or dilute the truth, while they enjoyed the personal fruits of good living and a certain fiscal comfort. This was especially true of the latter decades of Chapman's life and of Wood's time at Los Gatos, the home south of San Francisco that he shared with Sara Bard Field.[24] By that time he had a more stable financial situation.

Wood and the Underprivileged

Unlike some modern-day libertarians whose political theory starts and stops at their bank balance, Wood had a real concern for the value of all people. At the conclusion of his colorful speech to the Manhattan Club in 1902, he noted that

> ... the thing that brought about revolutions was the lack of the necessities of life, and that the people of the West and the poor of the East were today wondering if there was not something, somewhere, sometimes wrong in the system under which one man could gather millions and another

---

[24] See Chapman's essay "Politics," reprinted in *Unbought Spirit: A John Jay Chapman Reader* (Illinois 1998) for a shining discussion of what happens when a railroad wants to build in a small city.

by the hardest effort only make enough to eke out a bare existence.[25]

Modern libertarians would be well advised to consider Wood's thoughts about the proper balance of freedom and care for the larger social community.

An example of the extraordinary complexity of Wood's views and his knowledge of how societies work can be seen in this extract from *Why Strikes* (1907):

> There would never have been any revolutions if the upper classes had foreseen justice and wisely administered it in advance. The great corporations do not see that the slow and stupid creature called the Public will one day ask "Why should I wait while these people fight out their troubles? Have I no rights? Shall I, who have created this public corporation to serve me, be servant to my own creature?" So the public, tired of waiting for its telegrams and cars and branch line railways; tired of fattening multimillionaires with the dollars which should build new lines, improve old ones, increase wages, or reduce rates, will oust these private owners and take possession. The government ownership predicted by Mr. Bryan is sure to come. Much as I disbelieve in it in principle, much as I fear the vast army of government employees in an elective republic, I cannot blind myself to the fact that no single problem has been resolved on the side of individual freedom.

---

[25] This detail about the speech provided by Erskine Wood on pp. 98-99 of *Life of CESW*.

There were other warnings, for example his Memorial Day, 1893 speech in Portland, in which he reminded listeners that they should

> See to it, then, that rather than wealth, or fame or power you treasure the truth .... if there shall be such breeding as that, then we are safe; but if it shall be that all our men sacrifice their personal independence, their personal integrity, their personal convictions for the cold tampering with policy and profit, then I say, let us beware![26]

It seems clear that a basic concern with humanity undergirded much of what Wood said and did, and that his libertarian ideals were circumscribed by a recognition that people had to eat before they could make refined moral and political choices. At the same time, he tended to focus his time and energy on people of his own social class and lived as well as he could manage—often better than he could manage, hoping that the financial future could reimburse the indebted past.

Wood's View of Private Property

Wood's economic libertarianism did have a curious divergence when it came to real property, that is, land ownership. In brief, Wood did not believe in the legal concept of fee simple ownership, under which in theory a very small number of people can own all of the land and what it holds and pass it on via inheritance. He was particularly negative about unfettered inheritance of land, which he

---

[26] Quoted in Hamburger, *Two Rooms*, at p. 104.

viewed as taking away access to property rights from new generations. This is discussed in some detail in his Supreme Court skits (a segment of one of which is reprinted herein) and in *On Privilege*. Instead, he supported a doctrine of right and beneficial use. There is little doubt what his response would be to a recent study that considered the coming wave of inherited wealth:

> ... the boomers—at least those in the more affluent classes— are about to get yet another windfall. As the members of World War II's "Greatest Generation" die off, they are set to pass on between $8.4 trillion and $11.6 trillion to their Baby Boomer descendants, according to a study by MetLife. In the coming decades this tsunami of inherited money will likely accelerate class divisions, as those in the current top decile (in terms of income) gather in more than a million in parental bequests, while those in the lower class will at best count their inheritances in the thousands.

> Even as most younger Americans struggle to obtain decent jobs and secure property, the Welfare Institute concluded, America is moving toward an "inheritance-based economy" where access to the last generation's wealth could prove a critical determinant of both influence and power.[27]

In some of his writings Wood made clear that someone who actually made good use of land should be its *de facto* (and probably *de jure*) owner, rather than the land being owned by

---

[27] Joel Kotkin, Trustafarians Want to Tell You How to Live. *Daily Beast*, October 31, 2014.

an absentee rentier or distant corporation, though he was not personally an activist in the arena of land redistribution. This is made very clear in the conversation called *On Privilege*.

This concept is at variance with what we think of as a modern libertarian outlook, yet it fits within one strand of thinking associated with libertarian philosophy. Benjamin Tucker's writing in the late 19th Century included the idea that actual occupancy of land was necessary to maintain ownership rights and also opposed the idea that an absentee landlord could collect rent for land used by someone else.[28]

Likewise, tucked away in the beliefs and theories of economist Robert Nozick is the idea that only a property right whose provenance is untainted by injustice need be recognized by society. Thus rights asserted in property that was, at some point, acquired or perhaps even used unjustly could be decoupled from the current owner and, if the situs of the injustice was sufficiently clear, restored by way of restitution to the party against whom the unjust act was committed.

The natural destination of this approach to property rights is the view held by libertarian economist Murray Rothbard, whose absolutist views that land must be justly held or it can't be held at all are remarkably similar to Wood's.

These opinions do frighten the political horses, but the theory under which Native Americans and colonial-fringe peoples such as early Mexican settlers in the West are due more than what a faraway government gave them under the

---

[28] I am indebted to Brian Doherty's *Radicals for Capitalism* for helping to place Wood's thought in proper historical context. In particular his discussions of Tucker, Nozick and Rothbard explicate this distinctive side-channel of property-use theory.

terms of treaties they never saw surely has some virtue. The fact that many of these treaties were quickly abrogated, ignored and trashed during the western rush for gold and land may have rendered the issue of justly-held property of particular interest to Wood, whose relationship with Northwest tribes was personal and unique: Wood's son Erskine spent many months living with Chief Joseph's family and the connection between these families has remained remarkably vivid to this day.[29] This connection between Wood's interest in property law and his awareness of Native American rights appears in the mouth of a fictional Supreme Court Justice in the *Earthly Discourse* dialogue included here. Wood was also torn between his duty to his military superiors and his doubts about the way they treated Native peoples. This is apparent from his diaries and other writings, including unpublished drafts of poetry.[30]

There are many ways to construct layers of land ownership and land is but one factor in wealth and indeed in freedom. Consider the fictional system of *tanar* and *denerir* developed in some detail in Austin Tappan Wright's[31] novel *Islandia*, a relatively straightforward structure in which larger landowners share an agrarian space with other families in a legal and social relationship that includes certain mutual duties and rights. The *denerir*, a kind of dependent/tenant,

---

[29] See George Venn's "*Soldier to Advocate: C.E.S. Wood's 1877 Legacy.*"

[30] In addition to Venn's book, which sets forth some of these conflicts, see Wood's published journals in *Oregon Historical Quarterly* 70:5-38 (March 1969) and 70:139-170 (June 1969).

[31] Wright (1883-1931) was professor of law at the University of California at Berkeley (1916-1924) and the University of Pennsylvania (1924-1931).

had as much right to be on the physical property and use it for agrarian purposes as did the *tanar*. This was established by many hundreds of years of custom.

Wright was slightly younger than Wood but they came of age working within the same legal system and with many of the same social conditions. I suspect that Wood's distaste for class-based privileges and social distinctions would have resonated with Wright, whose Islandian culture was largely devoid of such trappings. *Islandia* was finally published in 1942, two years before Wood's death.

The idea of making the best use of land appears in many places in Wood's writings, but is set forth with enthusiasm and humor in some of the "Supreme Court" dialogues in *Earthly Discourse*:

SEVENTH ASSOCIATE JUSTICE: ... We talk of vested rights in property. There is no such thing. All property rights originated in either seizure by force or were bribed from or given by a sovereign power based on force—the State. Well, what was seized or given can be taken away for the common good when necessary. Only natural rights are perpetual as Nature is perpetual.

THE CHIEF JUSTICE: I feel it is time to say that I believe we would protect the Supreme Court, the People, Posterity, and ourselves as men, if we recognized in our minds that there is not a property right in the world that did not originate in seizure by force or by bribery and fraud or by grant as a special privilege from a sovereign established and ruling by force, though superstitiously called the Lord's Anointed. The whole feudal system was one of privileges and so-called rights, obtained by superior force or granted by overlords who by force and seizure owned from the center of the earth even to the sky. With us, Congress or the state legislature or city council has succeeded to these granters of rights. Congress or a state legislature or a city council is now the Lord's Anointed.

THE CLERK (Aside): Lord, have mercy upon us!

THE CHIEF JUSTICE: It is not very intelligent to believe that this planet and the machinery of society can be given to a few first comers, "their heirs and assigns forever," leaving the unborn generations disinherited, born into serfdom.

from Earthly Discourse, p. 158

FOURTH ASSOCIATE JUSTICE: This is Communism or something.

SIXTH ASSOCIATE JUSTICE: Think it out. The right to live is a natural right—a God-given right, and the right to live and seek happiness implies a right to share the God-given means whereby to live and to be happy. Can you imagine how anyone—feudal lord or modern State—has a right to give away the unborns' right to live and to have a just share in the happiness of living? There can be no absolutely vested rights in property. It is a foolish and a feudal idea: chiefly entertained by modern barons and the utterly ignorant.

THE CLERK (Aside): With us, the most valuable natural and social monopolies have been granted, for a lobbied price, to shrewd forestallers who preferred the peaceful "lawful" predatory way of corrupt and corrupting lobbies and corrupt and corrupting legislation, approved by the Supreme Court.

SIXTH ASSOCIATE JUSTICE: Lucky for us that the cave dwellers or the American Indians did not know enough to set up a feudal system of overlords and feudal grants to "A. B., his heirs and assigns forever!" We would all be serfs by this time.

THE CLERK (Aside): And the Supreme Court, five to four, would be straining to protect those sacred vested, ripened rights—so ripened they are rotten.

SEVENTH ASSOCIATE JUSTICE: It's all bosh about these vested rights, inviolable for all eternity. They are privileges—given or stolen—and that is why the privileged are so fearful of any change. What were the sacred inviolable rights of Southern slaveholders? What are the inviolable rights of a farmer to his farm and his home if a railroad or a power corporation happens to want them?

SECOND ASSOCIATE JUSTICE: That's the exercise of eminent domain. It is legal.

SEVENTH ASSOCIATE JUSTICE: We should be careful how we lift that scarecrow "legal." Slaves were once legal. Crowns were once legal.

from Earthly Discourse, p. 159-160

SIXTH ASSOCIATE JUSTICE: The Past! That's just it! The dead fetter the living. The men who wrote that Constitution were no more able to decide for us today than we are able now to lay down the unalterable laws of

Medes and Persians to control the people of two hundred years hence, and to compel the solution of their problems by our knowledge, our theories. As has been said, not a man in that Constitutional Convention was of the working class, the middle class, or of the common people—not one. The Constitution is a document for the privileged class, and the Bill of Rights inserted by Madison and Jefferson is a dead letter. Yes, Justice Holmes said the United States would survive without either Constitution or Supreme Court. I am with him. Give me a form of government not fettered by any written constitution, not ordered by whispers from the tomb—a form of government which, as Lord Birkenhead said, leaves a free people absolutely free to work out their own salvation, free to make their own mistakes and free to correct them, and thus by experience to develop in a natural order of evolution. No mistakes are very bad when the way is open to intelligent correction with all the value of experience.

from Earthly Discourse, p. 170

How could this point of view be expressed, in terms of political economy? It is clearly Wood's own view, as it appears in various guises in other writings. It is not anarchy; it is a kind of incomplete redistributive philosophy—incomplete because nowhere does Wood propose (or work toward) a fully realized social mechanism to actually move from the way property is conceived now in the United States toward what he thinks the norm should be. He in effect cherry-picked something he thought good policy from socialism without preparing any ground in which to plant it.

Upon visiting England, I was surprised to discover that the "easement" concept, under which certain rights of access and use of property by a non-owner are allowed, was much more developed there than in the U.S. Perhaps developed is the wrong word, for the right that allows someone to walk from Cambridge to Grantchester using a well-trodden path through a private pasture is a very old right, not a modern overlay by politically obstreperous nature-lovers. It is a custom like the rights of the *denerir*, but one enshrined in law as much as the trees are in their meadow. Wood's conception of property is a far more extreme idea, yet there are certain parallels, among which is the idea of how to best use a given physical space.

A Note on States and Individuals

In *Too Much Government*, Wood often speaks of the importance of state governments and local government as superior in various ways to the federal government. One of the curiosities of this aspect of Wood's commentary is that he, one of the great 20th Century champions of the individual, should in one section [32] of *Too Much Government* refer, presumably, to the content of the 10th Amendment as though it only reserved certain powers to the *states*. That amendment actually reads "The powers not delegated to the United States by the Constitution, nor prohibited by it to the States, are reserved to the States respectively, or *to the people*." (emphasis added). It may be that for him the states and the

---

[32] See p. 152, referring to p. 143-145 of TMG.

people were one, at the time, or perhaps by comparison to the relationship between the people and the federal government.

❖ Social Freedoms ❖

Today we take at least a modest amount of sexual freedom for granted, but even now I suspect that the freewheeling sexuality of C.E.S. Wood would arouse comment. He started out as a reasonably standard Victorian-era American male, marrying a respectable woman (Nannie Moale Smith) and having children. However, over time he broadened his intimate relations outside his marriage. This is not uncommon among men, but Wood's attitude was unusually relaxed and open given the social norms of the early 20th Century. His ideas were sufficiently visible and distinctive that other writers took note, as when John Bowman used Wood as an example in his book *Socialism in America*:

> In this respect "middle class morality" is that which enables a society to exist, and the upper class intellectuals who believe they are above it can behave as such only because the middle class continues to believe and comply with moral imperatives. This makes conspicuous the upper class intellectual's game, like CES Wood's, which is essentially libertarian. They advance those ideas that enable them to do what they want. Wood believes in freedom because he wants to have freedom to be sexually promiscuous without society's disapprobation.[33]

---

[33] John Bowman, *Socialism in America* (2005), p. xx.

Relationships with Sara Bard Field and others

Wood began a relationship with Sara Bard Field Ehrgott in Portland when they were both married to other people (he to Nannie and she to the Rev. Albert Ehrgott), and that relationship overcame various forms of opposition, both formal and informal, through practice and the passage of time. Very little is said by commentators about the age difference in the relationship, which was thirty years—they met when Wood was 58 and Field 28. It may be that such differences, absent an existing marriage, simply did not arouse much comment at the time; it is likely that today there would be more eyebrows raised at the age difference than at the relative marital status of the partners.

In his formal writings there were occasional references to sexual freedoms, especially in later life, but while he was married to his first wife Nannie his comment on such issues was usually limited and circumspect. However, even in those years he sometimes allowed his thoughts to emerge in poetry, as in a flowery and curiously lumbering poem for Sara, with whom he spent the final decades of his life:

LXVIII

From freedom comes our growth and all our good.
    I know how deep your soul has hungered it,
Just to be free in a bound, stupid, rude
    And too intrusive world. To, musing, sit
Weaving the fabric of your fantasy;
    Joying in creation-lust. Creator thou;
Rich in the rustless ores of poesy;
    Slaking your soul-thirst in the nectared Now.
As humming-birds the honeysuckle suck,
    We will rejoice in rains which make the flowers;
From thistles we'll the purple blossoms pluck,
    Toss garlands on the free, unfettered hours.
So you shall find from sordid bonds release,
And in my arms the sure and perfect peace.[34]

This work is typical of Wood's poetry in that it combines excessively colorful and sometimes clumsy language with occasional flashes of superlative poetry, e.g. "rustless ores," the "nectared Now" and the simple loveliness of the perfectly paced final couplet.

Wood's ideas about free love and the nature of intimate commitments are discussed in an interesting paper[35] about the history and kinds of free love. One section discusses Wood's ideas of sexual freedoms thus:

---

[34] From the privately printed collection called *Maia* (1918).
[35] See *Luisa Capetillo and Charles Erskine Scott Wood: Free Love and the State at the Turn of the Twentieth Century.*
Polywog blog, http://polywog.wordpress.com/luisa-capetillo-and-charles-erskine-scott-wood-free-love-and-the-state-at-the-turn-of-the-twentieth-century/

Sara and Erskine had such a profound love for each other as to triumph over many people's discomforts with their free love beliefs. Historian Christine Stansell documents Wood's "long line of lovers" as follows: "his secretary; fellow members of the local branch of the Socialist Party; a New Womanish physician; his wife; and the feminist Sara Bard Field, his longest-lasting, longest-suffering, and most obsessively devoted lover (she outlasted all competition and eventually became his second wife)." But to label Sara as obsessively devoted to Erskine is to tell a story one sided. The two were by all evidence equally devoted, and it was not outlasting competition which caused the two to marry, but only the legalities of growing old. In Robert Hamburger's words, Wood realized that:

> "his unconventional relationship with Sara might lead to legal problems that could keep her from receiving the substantial legacy he had provided for her. After fifty years of arguing that government had no province over love and sexual union, Wood remarried."

Contrary to Stansell's depiction, Sara and Erskine's 1938 wedding actually celebrated free love. Their rabbi included important anti-authoritarian sentiments in his service:

> "I would feel myself sacrilegiously presumptuous to feel that I, as an individual, had any divine authority to pronounce you husband and wife. Your lives have done that in a manner that has been an example of true marriage far more powerfully than the lives of many whose marriage was, from the first, legalized."

Stansell accurately finds that

> "free love justified his excursions outside marriage and at
> the same time allowed him to hold on to marriages
> safeties. In a peculiarly fin-de-siècle manner, he melded
> anarchist tenets of personal liberty, Romantic sonorities
> about Truth and Beauty, and a lyrical celebration of
> female sexual power... to embellish his seductions and
> betrayals with higher morality."[36]

Wood's relationship with Sara Bard Field and the legal
machinations surrounding it are at the core of an article
about changing patterns of divorce by Glenda Riley.[37]
Although the article is concerned mainly with the advent of
new norms regarding divorce in the early 20th Century, it also
contains some thoughts about Wood and Field's specific
situation. Regarding their transition to living together, Riley
writes

> He and Sara Field established a home together in San
> Francisco, an action that elicited a range of opinions from
> Sara's family. Sara's eldest child Albert, a young adolescent
> five years older than his sister Kay, wrote to Wood: "I hope
> that it won't be so very long now when people who love
> each other will not have to have a few silly damn fool

---

[36] From Polywog's *Luisa Capetillo and Charles Erskine Scott Wood: Free Love
and the State at the Turn of the Twentieth Century*, citing Christine Stansell,
"Talking About Sex: Early-Twentieth-Century Radicals and Moral
Confessions" in *Moral Problems in American Life: New Perspectives on Cultural
History*, ed. Karen Halttunen and Lewis Perry, (New York: Cornell
University Press, 1998), 288

[37] Sara Bard Field, Charles Erskine Scott Wood, and the Phenomenon of
Migratory Divorce, Glenda Riley, *California History* Vol. 69, No. 3 (Fall,
1990), pp. 250-259.

words said over them by a parson to make them a so-called husband and wife." Albert added that he had never seen "a love so great and wonderful and beautiful" as that shared by his mother and Wood.

Ehrgott[38] also wrote to Wood, but in a very different tone. He told Wood that his "dribbling philosophy of free love is but a futile excuse for an unholy indulgence of love and a sacrilegious intrusion into another man's home which aroused public conscience will not much longer tolerate." Ehrgott accused Wood of stealing another man's wife, trifling with God, and defying public opinion and morals. ...

Erhgott was mistaken about the public's conscience and opinions. As Americans entered the second decade of the twentieth century, they were more committed than ever to democracy, individualism, and the right of citizens to make decisions about their own lives as long as their actions did not harm others. As a result, a new code of morality gained adherents, as the anti-divorce arguments of religious leaders, moralists, and conservative reformers lost ground. At the same time, a growing number of articles in magazines and newspapers supported the idea of divorce as a positive act and an American citizen's prerogative.

Thus is Wood's attitude about sexual freedom (and Field's) placed in some historical context. On Wood's attitude toward restrictive moralities, Riley notes that

---

[38] Sara Bard Field's husband at the time, Rev. Albert Ehrgott.

In 1927, Wood put his philosophy of marriage into words when he wrote to his estranged son Erskine in an attempt to explain his and Field's relationship. Wood optimistically wrote of his belief that "old, narrow and early crude conventions" based on the "right of possession and the justness of jealousy" were breaking down and that "conventions founded on the right of every individual to his own soul and his own life" were gradually replacing the older notions. The "old idea of the sacrament of marriage" was fading as well, because so many marriages ended in "shipwrecks." If marriage was based upon the "mutual love of the parties and the mutual desire for companionship and mutual willingness to live together" then, "when this mutual desire to live together ends," the marriage relation also ends. To Wood, it was unethical to force two people to live together "against the will of either." He was baffled that so many people failed to see that freedom to part was "best for society and the race," that every couple forced to remain together despite altered feelings was "a cancer," and that "every refusal of freedom leads to falsities." Wood swore that he and Field would never marry; their refusal to marry would be their protest against "the archaic superstition and falsity" known as marriage.

Many years later, they did marry, after Wood's heart attack caused concern about the future of their property.

Wood's attitude toward homosexuality

In addition to his growing commitment to free love, inspired by his own situation, Wood also wrote a broad-minded defense of homosexual people, an unusual view at the time, in *Too Much Government* (1931). The context was a comment on whether certain books were obscene. It is set forth in part below; the full quotation from *TMG* appears later in this volume.

> It is a great curse, as is any abnormality. How great a curse—how difficult and hopeless a situation—only the scientists and the victims know. It is a blunder of Nature that calls for all the pity we are capable of. Every reasonably well-informed person now knows that this abnormality is not obscene, but is a most pathetic phase of human life, quite common; and its study and its tragedy are as much the fit subject of art as they are of science. To read about it or see a drama founded on it will no more corrupt the young than to see *Macbeth* or *Hamlet*. The subject is a study in human psychology and suffering, as jealousy is, or any other mania; and to see such a play or read such a book can no more make a person a homosexualist than it can make a man a woman, or a woman a man. The "making" is done before birth; in the laboratory of our bungling old Mother.[39]

To a modern eye, this defense may seem crude, harsh and devoid of warmth, yet considering the time period in which this was written and what was known about sexual orientation then, Wood's understanding that sexual orientation is at least in part of genetic origin was ahead of its time.

Not much was known about the origins of homosexuality when Wood wrote. Havelock Ellis's work with John Symonds had appeared in German in 1896 and as *Sexual Inversion* in English in 1897, clothed as a medical textbook, though it

---

[39] *Too Much Government*, pp. 110-111.

achieved some general notice. Some of Sigmund Freud's work on male sexuality appeared in 1905. André Gide's first widespread publication of *Corydon* was in 1924 and Kinsey's report "*Sexual Behavior in the Human Male*" (1949) was eighteen years in the future from the date *TMG* appeared.

It seems likely that Wood arrived at his views of homosexuality through the simple fact of knowing some gay people and being aware of how their lives functioned. He would have been unusually aware of the subject because Portland had seen an extraordinary local scandal in 1912-13 involving the exposure of local gay people and their ways of life. This would have been well-known to Wood and he knew some of those involved.[40] Wood ran in the same political circles as, for example, homosexual lawyer Edward Stonewall Jackson McAllister, one of the more prominent figures in the scandal.

Wood and McAllister were both active in the Single Tax League, of which McAllister was an officer. As McAllister's trial went forward and his career collapsed subsequent to his sodomy conviction (later overturned), one can imagine Wood, who had worked with him on some important cases, feeling some purely human sensitivity and sorrow for the fate of someone with whom he had shared much in the community (see Boag, 1999, for more details on this interesting event and pioneer-era sexuality issues).

---

[40] For more information on the Portland sex scandals, see Peter Boag, "Sex & Politics in Progressive-Era Portland and Eugene: The Local Response to the 1912 Same-Sex Vice Scandal." *Oregon Historical Quarterly* 100:2 (Summer 1999), 158-181. For a larger discussion of regional attitudes toward homosexuality in historical context, see Boag's *Same-Sex Affairs: Constructing and Controlling Homosexuality in the Pacific Northwest.* Berkeley: University of California Press, 2003.

Wood's notions of free love, while expansive, did not clearly extend to homosexual relations, although he made clear that he considered maltreatment of people because they were gay to be wrong. His approach seems to be that because such people were in some way naturally flawed, they should be treated with kindness and understanding, not contempt.

Works of C.E.S. Wood

C.E.S. *Wood*, 1892

Imperialism vs. Democracy

An Address at the Jefferson Birthday Dinner,
Portland, Oregon, April 13, 1899.
The Pacific Monthly 2, (May-October 1899): 57-68.

President and Fellow Democrats:

I am glad I am here tonight. I am glad we are once more a united family, and I am grateful for that delicate tact which refrained from putting on the bill of fare either husks or veal.

We have differed in the past; we shall differ in the future, but unless we can allow to each other the privilege of independence we are not true democrats. If we cannot sit at table with those who do not think as we think, we are not true gentlemen.

Speaking for the future as well as for the past, I say let us remember kindly our friends who with an honesty as great as our own cannot view the political situation as we view it. I despise the man who arrogates to himself all the honesty and wisdom of the occasion.

I do not know who selected my subject, but the very title printed on this card is both the text and the sermon—

"Imperialism vs. Democracy," Imperialism, Emperor, Imperator, Commander, vs. Democracy—the people. Militarism versus the people. This new path that opens up before the Republic—this "expansion" as it is called may be examined in two lights—the selfish and the moral.

Following what seems to be the fashion of the administration I shall put the selfish first.

Expediency.

Is it good and profitable for us to have the Philippines? Place the Filipinos wholly to one side, as our worthy President seems to have done, and let us look at it wholly in our own selfish interests as a free Republic of free voters and free homemakers.

More than three thousand years ago there was in Greece a democracy. I know it did not have our matured system, the divisions of governmental power—our so-called checks and balances. But have our checks and balances preserved the senate in its integrity? Has there not been a steady increase in executive influence? My dear sirs, liberty was never preserved by any checks and balances ever invented. The stock and stamina and independence of the individual are the guardians of liberty and the price of liberty is eternal vigilance.

In the Grecian democracy every free man was a voter. The bravery of the Rough Riders was not greater than that of those who stood at Thermopylae. The world has not since seen sculptors equal to Phidias or Praxiteles, nor heard singers more divine than Homer, sweeter than Theocritus or more impassioned than Sappho.

It is true Christ was not yet. It is true something has been done in steam, electricity and science, but these are not the bulwarks of liberty. Liberty and slavery lie in human nature itself. Have we among us a wiser than Socrates or Plato or Aristotle?

Because we know more of microbes and the asteroids, are we politically a braver, shrewder or more liberty-jealous people than the Greeks? Alexander pushed his conquests in seven years to the Punjaub and set up the emblems between Lahore and Delhi. The known world was conquered and the brave wise commonwealth that began with annexation and colonization, and expansion ended in conquest and imperialism and today the archaeologist digs for the remnants of that empire and the Parthenon is in ruins upon the Acropolis. Rome stood upon her seven hills and looked upon the known world in vassalage at her feet. Every Roman citizen was a king more regally and truly than is the citizen of the United States today. Citizenship was freely extended to the cities and provinces that were absorbed by the great republic, and during its early growth the republic was the home of free men making their own laws and electing their own executive.

But Rome, the great republic, Rome, the free commonwealth, Rome, the sovereignty of the people, pushed her provinces to the uttermost verge—from France and Great Britain to Africa and India—she too broke with her own weight and lies buried in the dust. The provinces and the frontier made the legions necessary. The legions became the masters, and the throne of Rome was sold to the highest bidder.

It is said our age is different. The spirit of our age makes long liberty possible. That seems to me the song of the fool soothing himself with his folly. Has the spirit of our age wiped out all selfishness from the human heart? Has it destroyed ambition or lust of power or love of wealth, of luxury? Has it truly leveled all classes and changed the human heart? Has it abolished poverty and dependence?

What are we with our little single century that we should forget Rome's thirteen centuries of glory and decay! Is Marcus Aurelius McKinley wiser than Marcus Aurelius the good? or than Pertinax? Do we build better than Rome did? or make finer roads or acqueducts? The whole world today is governed by the code of laws, wise and just, which Rome gave to the world, and the harsh law of the Anglo-Saxon has been conquered by the equitable principles of Roman law. Every religion was freely tolerated and protected by Rome. I say this notwithstanding the later persecution of the Christians for political reasons.

Have we better men than Cicero, Cato, Seneca? Have we braver regiments than the Roman legions? Has Christian toleration and love of our fellow man swept away all corruption, all selfishness and tyranny,—Has it? I call the miners of Pennsylvania and Illinois to witness. I call to witness the Standard Oil Company, the Pennsylvania railroad, the Sugar Trust, the legislatures of Pennsylvania, Utah, Ohio, Washington, California, Oregon and the United States senate, and lastly I call to witness the "rebel" Filipinos. Where the rebel Filipinos are today, under the armed heel, your descendants may be an hundred years hence.

France, thirsty for expansion, pushed her eagles to Moscow. France, with her doctrine of equality and liberty and the rights of man, France became imperial and expanded, and the Napoleonic empire passed away and Europe fell back into its just bounds as swollen streams subside. Today France is a republic, groaning under militarism, and yet this is our own Christian era. Where is the Spirit of the Age?

Germany is ruled by a despot, asserting still the God-given right of kings— the royal flesh superior in essence to the peasant flesh—and Germany sends her peasants to their work each with an armed soldier on his back, or on her back, for the women work to support the army. The army loafs to support the Crown, and the excuse for this is the boundary line between France and Germany. Into this question of boundaries, of sovereign rights and duties, into all this muddle of the "Family of Nations," we, poor fools, are rushing headlong without sense to see that we have grown and become great, not so much from a special divinity in ourselves, but we have lived in a land of boundless resources and a land wholly cut off from the wars and rumors of wars of Europe. We have been left peacefully to grow and wax fat on a continent of our own. It seems to me that he is an enemy to our peace and happiness that desires to force upon us this festering sore, the Philippines.

We have heard tonight from an eloquent and honored speaker that Jefferson was the first great expansionist. That is but little to me. Truth speaks for itself, and error would not be less error to me because Jefferson spoke it. But we all know in our inner hearts that warding off friction on our continent is entirely different from going seven thousand miles to sea to hunt up a fight. Taking in territory that is actually contiguous to us, thus preventing boundary frictions hereafter, thus preparing suitable homes on our own continent for our growing people, absorbing a people of our own blood, if not our own language, is very different from stretching our boundary uselessly seven thousand miles to sea, to take in a tropical island with an Asiatic population of mixed blood, and a very bone of contention in the "Family of Nations."

Jefferson made the Louisiana purchase. It was wise then; it is still wise; but if Jefferson stood here tonight, I must believe he would raise his warning finger and pointing to the hem of our Pacific shores, he would say, "Halt!" The conjuring of Jefferson as an expansionist, viewed in the light of the two situations, seems to me such nonsense that it will impress those only who already are convinced.

But Jefferson's name is used to father everything. He is placarded as favoring the unlimited power of the Supreme Court of the United States, when it is common history that he hated John Marshall, Chief Justice, to his dying day, for what Jefferson thought was his usurpation of power by the Court in vetoing the acts of Congress and interfering in state affairs. He is called the champion of free silver at 16 to 1, when it ought to be common school knowledge that he declared the ratio to be a commercial problem altogether, and so actually treated it in his own practice.

The point is not what Jefferson said, or Washington said; it is what is essentially true in itself. And what is essentially true is generally pretty well understood in our hearts, even though we selfishly argue ourselves away from it. So we return to our question, Is expansion good for us? It would seem as if the course of every nation heretofore has been this expansion complication, a necessary military establishment. Militarism— the masses held down by the organized armed force— despotism, decay.

Are we to be exempt? We are very young yet. Six thousand years ago, if the Pharaoh standing by the lisping edge of the Nile, had tossed a handful of sand into the air, it would have fallen to the ground. Twenty thousand years ago the waters of the Nile were flowing from the mountain to the sea. The law that brings the sand back to the ground and the water of the mountains to the sea is the same today, and if I tried to prove to you that water always runs down hill, you would say I was wasting time.

Yet when I suggest that this free, enlightened, wealthy, powerful young republic of ours, if it sows the same seeds that Greece, Rome and Venice sowed, will reap the same harvest; that the same causes that turned Greece and Rome into despotisms for the joy of a governing class at the expense of the man of the people, will produce the same effect in the

United States, I am met with derisive laughter, and our friends of the other side say, "Why this solemn mouthing over a paltry army of one hundred thousand men and a few islands in mid-ocean?"

My God! Do you not realize that the easiest victim is he who is most confident in his strength. There would be no decay, no downfall, no despotism if it came boldly, suddenly, and aroused the hatred and the fears of the people. But it comes as the leaves are now coming on the dogwoods and maples. No one sees them grow, no one can mark any change from day to day, and yet in six weeks behold the bud has changed to the full leaf. Or, rather, it comes as a disease that creeps upon its victim so gradually that by the time he is aware that he is tainted, he is doomed.

I am used to being called a pessimist, a screech-owl, a fool, a traitor, a copperhead, and those other names bestowed by our adversaries upon those who do not think with them, but I believe abuse is not argument, nor epithets logic. I believe a man can be as much a patriot in uttering his honest belief that his country is wrong, as he who persuades her to become a harlot among nations.

I believe he is deserving of a statue of bronze who will teach the people of the United States they are but men; that they are not a new Israel, the chosen of a God who will save them from their own folly; that they must suffer the consequences of their violations of the laws of truth and morality just precisely as the pagan nations did.

Which do we regard as the greatest patriots in England in 1776, Burke and Chatham, who lashed England for her persecution of her colonies, or those Tories that applauded Lord North and the Stamp Act? Who dares say Edmund Burke was a copperhead and a traitor?

What is this spirit of the age? This destiny of the American people which are to save us as Rome was not saved?

Has our Constitution ever been proof against the demand of the prevailing party for the moment? What of the greenback legal tender decision? What of the income tax decisions? What of the Force Bill? Has the spirit of the age prevented greed and oppression and wars in Russia, Turkey, France, Germany, Greece, Finland? Has there, or has there not, been any tendency in this country to separate the classes from the masses? Is the poor voter as free and independent today as in the origin of this government?

You will be told that there always will be such howling pessimists as I, that they croaked in Washington's time. Well, I say, if they foresaw the difference between then and now, they had cause to croak. It is useless to say this country has not grown less free, more under the boss rule as it has grown more wealthy and more popular. It is true, and we know it is true. Today instead of being as it was then, purely a government of the people, by the people, for the people, it is a government of the people by the politicians for the bosses.

I do not pretend that this is not today a free country, a great country, a good country to live in. I want to keep it so, not for my time, but for all time, for longer than the thirteen centuries of Rome, and I say as I look in the rapid changes since Jefferson's time, I am afraid to give the bosses and their hungry horde any foothold on Asiatic Islands, with the coolie laborers. I am afraid to give them any excuse for a great army and navy. I remember the great Roman Empire and its Senate were dominated by only twenty thousand armed men—the Praetorian Guards.

Organized armed force is a power irresistible by the unorganized and unsupported mob. I am afraid to give any further excuse for taxation. I do not want to see our men and women going to work with soldiers on their backs. I was in the army myself, and I tell you the idea of discipline and loyalty to orders is the one dominant idea. I claim to be an educated man. I was born a democrat, and yet when I was in the army I would have executed any order whatever; I might have questioned, but I would not have disobeyed.

That is a spirit dangerous to the Republic. We want as little of it as possible. It is obedience, not love for the job, that keeps our soldiers in the Philippines. It is for the Nation to do the thinking; the soldiers can only obey. Eternal vigilance is the price of liberty! I may be croaking far ahead of the time, but better croak now than when too late. The beginnings are always trifles. This is as true in politics as it is of the Columbia river. I may be a goose, but Rome was saved by the cackling of geese.

I have no idea the offensive word King will ever be heard in this land. I have no idea our forms of government and election will ever be changed, but for centuries after it was the most absolute of monarchies, Rome preserved all the forms of the republic. It is always so. The senate was so jealous of its form that it remained the elective and legislative body in form long after it was in fact the veriest machine for registering every insane wish of the Emperor backed by his Praetorians. Today in electing a senator is a legislature the free representative of a free people, or is it a mere creature to do the will of the machine boss?

The only rebellion we ever witness is the struggle between rival factions. The people are unthought-of and unheard. We shall not be offended by crowns and thrones, a royal family or an hereditary presidency. It is not necessary. Mexico is governed and they say well governed by a president elected regularly by himself under cover of his army. The forms are all gone through with, but nevertheless they are mere forms and Diaz is an absolute monarch.

The forms we now have, popular ballot, congress and a president, will be left to amuse us as children play with a stuffed rag in the likeness of a doll. But given Asiatic colonies to furnish coolie worked plantations to our Quays and our Crokers and their carpet-baggers, to our Huntingtons and their syndicates; given a large army and navy under the orders of the executive; given the increased patronage for colonial possessions, and I, myself, as supreme boss, would undertake less than a hundred years hence not only to leave the empty forms to the American people, but to have them powerless within my grasp till revolution might set them free. Therefore, I shall, while I live, still call aloud the watch cry and kindle the alarm fires; still beg my fellow citizens to believe we are not the only republic that ever existed, not the only nation of free men that ever lived, not the only community where the common man was the voter and ostensible origin of power.

I will tell them there are nations dead and gone that had laws, commerce, literature, science, civil and religious liberty as well as we; that there have been on the earth nations that were as proud in their own conceit as we and with as much reason: that these also talked of destiny and thought themselves the chosen instruments of God. And I shall tell them that the historian shall hereafter write of us:

These people were a brave, intelligent, prosperous race, with a land three thousand miles from ocean to ocean, having every climate and resource known to the temperate zone. They were far removed from the clash of arms and were outside of the whirlpool of the old world, yet at the very instant their social and political conditions required their closest attention to prevent the encroachment of wealth and concentrated power upon the liberties of the common man they became mad and blind from greed which, they persuaded themselves, was honor, and led by the leaders they should have most feared they plunged into the eddies of European politics. They grasped at some Asiatic Islands which became mere farms worked by coolies for the wealthy classes and political bosses. Above all, they violated their pure and fixed traditions and gave an excuse to the clever politician for increased armies and navies and greater taxation. They furnished a ready means by which their attention could be distracted from their discontent at home, and any tendency to domestic revolt could be suppressed, and the beginning of the end may be dated from the conquest of the United States by Spain in selling to the republic for twenty millions of dollars the Philippine Islands and the inhabitants thereof.

I say the historian who shall write this will close his chapter with the words, "Fools and Blind!"

So I am opposed to this imperialism because I believe it is opposed to every element of our natural life, and is but the first step on the old, old race for glory, gain and power—the path by which a few have risen and by which the people have gone down.

There is still another selfish argument. This country is a country of the plain people, for the plain people. It is the fashion nowadays in secret to sneer at the ignorance of the common laborer, though in the campaign the same man who sneers in private will prate of the wonderful intelligence of the plain working man—just as some lawyers fawn over a jury to their faces and then damn them behind their backs. I myself feel alarm as I see the increasing army of sots and bums and benighted foreigners who offer for sale in the cities that priceless pearl of citizenship, a freeman's vote. When I think of all the blood and treasure and the agony of noble souls that has been offered as the price for this precious freedom, I would be willing to have the sot that sells it thrown into the sea.

But, gentleman, thank God! the great man of the American people is not yet so low or so enslaved—not yet is this scum vote the balance of power. Still on the farms and in the workshops are men as jealous of their birthright and as intelligent to use it in a moral question as any in the land.

If I could believe that to the American working man the Philippines would open up a new field, I might on the question of selfish expediency believe we ought to enlarge our domain. But to my eyes it is clear that this expansion folly will not give a brighter hope to any man with a dinner bucket. More than that, it will increase his present burdens, and put a heavier shackle on his heavy limbs.

Who are the colonizing nations of modern times? First and foremost Great Britain; second, Holland. The mother country sent her sons to America and Australia and they have out of the wildernesses in the temperate zones builded themselves new nations. But in the tropics, among the coolie civilizations of Asia, what has the white man done? Show me in India, in China, in Java, in the Straits, settlements anywhere one village of white men, one factory or yard or farm with white laborers! There is not one. The white laborer cannot compete with the native coolie, who lives on nothing, works for nothing and is content to be an abject beast of burden.

In the dock yards in Hong Kong are 8,000 employes, all Chinamen or Asiatics, save six overseers. The cooks, the nurses, the housemaids, the horses, the porters, the farm hands, in India, Java, Hong Kong, everywhere in Asia are natives. The white men are there to govern. That is all. They are of the civil service or the military service. The Philippines will open to a few political pets a place for salaries. To a few merchant princes a place to work coolies. To a few army officers a new field, and to a few saloonkeepers a new stand among the vices of the tropics; but to the self-respecting white laborer it offers nothing—absolutely nothing to him or to his children.

The Island of Java is worked by the Dutch for the Dutch, but it does not mean the Dutch people. There is not a white laborer in the island. But there are twenty-six governors of provinces at ten thousand dollars a year, each. Not only is there no place in all the Indian possessions for a British workingman, but he would be despised if he did work. Labor and the sweat of the brow in those lands is left with contempt to the cringing coolies. If this was a country organized for a privileged class, if it was a country having a nobility and a governing order that were recognized as having a superior right to the riches and power of this world, we, too, might annex some Asiatic coolie farms: but the very birth cry of this nation in its infant agony was that it was to be a nation of the people and for the people.

A new territory, then, which does not open up as much to the American laborer as it does to any one else is not a territory for us to acquire benevolently or violently, or at all.

The pretense of our doing right in this conquest of ours is frankly abandoned by some who say "trade follows the flag"—I deny it. If Oregon and California were separate nations, would it alter their trade with each other? Would it alter their trade with Alaska if Alaska was a colony of Oregon? Not a particle, unless laws were made by Oregon discriminating against California, for trade follows the price. The lowest price to the buyer will get all the trade if the door be open. Do we want to perpetuate our beautiful protective system, that takes from the pockets of the people a bonus for the manufacturer? Do we want to extend to these islands our Trust-creating folly?

This thing of "trade following the flag" seems to me mere bald assertion. In heaven's name what is there in the flag that would induce Manila to pay us more for cotton cloth or steel hatches than Manchester can sell them for - Or, if we can undersell Manchester, what is there to prevent our controlling the Manila trade?

For many of the following facts I am indebted to a pamphlet by Mr. John J. Valentine, entitled "Imperial Democracy." I now quote some of his figures. He shows by tables taken from the Stateman's Year Book, that from 1893 to 1897 inclusive, Great Britain lost 200 millions export trade to her own colonies. The United States gained 270 millions exports to foreign markets. The same is true in less amounts with Germany, Holland and France. He also shows that M. Peletan, reporting to the French Chamber, showed a cost to

France of her colonies of 90 millions of dollars and a net loss of 60 millions.

But the army follows the flag. The navy follows the flag. Taxation follows the flag; and the speculator, the government contractor, the bond-buyer, they follow the flag. And in cost of governing we are doing well already.

It is estimated by those long resident in the Philippines that to maintain order there will cost us one hundred millions a year. General Lawton's estimate is 100,000 men for the Philippines. The annual cost of a soldier in this country is $1,000 a year. To this must be added cost of transports and added expenses incident to foreign service.

The above estimates include nothing for civil government, the expenses of which must come from the Filipinos themselves. The best year of Philippine trade shows a gross value of $30,000,000, of which $20,000,000 is exports from the islands and $10,000,000 is imports. The United States, of course, has only a share of this $10,000,000. Besides the international complications our possession of the Philippines will lead to, it is evident a vast burden will be laid upon our own people or the Filipinos for the benefit of a few army contractors, rope-makers and ship-owners.

How the great common mass of the American people are to be benefited by either the outgo or the income, is a mystery to me, except that the surplus sons of the poor can be drawn off into the foreign army.

To pensioners last year we paid nearly $146,000,000. The cost of running this free and economical government will, for 1899, probably exceed that of any other nation in the world. We pity Germany under her military burden without realizing that we pay as pensions more than it costs Germany to maintain her army. The fact is this country is being eaten up by political locusts and the Philippines will be the fattening field for a favored few.

We all have friends out there. Read their letters—what do even the young and reckless soldiers say? They say the climate is hell; that no one can work but Chinese and Japanese and Malays; that the Chinese own most of the trade, shops and farms; that but a small part of the island is settled or civilized. I despise an American who is afraid to die, but the Philippines are not worth dying for, unless some great principle is at stake.

Morality.

Let us now turn to the moral side of the question and see what great principle is at stake. I do not believe every moral transgression brings immediate punishment. *He who lives by the sword does not always die by the sword, but his seed does.*[41] *I do believe, however, take all the ages together, that a breach of the true moral law works out its own retribution as surely as does a breach of the laws of health.* Thomas Jefferson, thinking of slavery, said: "I tremble for my country when I remember that God is just."

---

[41] The passage shown in italics is garbled in the original printed version. I have stitched the lines together in the way that makes the most sense.

How easy would have been the abolition of slavery then. But how pleasant and how safe it seemed to let the stars and stripes cast its flickering shadow on a slave. The Declaration of Independence and slavery could not stand together and the Declaration of Independence was the moral law, the truth eternal. It worked out its own vengeance. Such a whirlwind of gloom and desolation, such a deluge of fraternal blood as left no doubt but that every day of slavery had been adding its own burden to the dreadful debt.

O! My brethren and my fellow citizens, we are no monarchy of Europe, we are no lingering despotism of the world, we are ourselves, alone, peculiar. We were not born to govern others against their will. We were born to carry freedom, not fetters. Our boast has been not that we can subdue the feeble nations to an easy vassalage, but that all men are created equal, and there is no just law under heaven, save by consent of the governed. I had rather this young republic of the free never stretched her borders one foot beyond her sea girt shores and chosen boundaries, than that she became mistress of the world by treason to her noble creed. Better that she conquer her own spirit than that she subdue to a sordid harvest the distant savage praying for freedom.

Aye! I would rather see her wiped off the face of the map and the Star Spangled Banner folded away, so that she went down battling to the last as at the first for freedom, liberty, the right of the people to choose their own government.

The argument that we mean well is nothing; so did the Spanish inquisition. The Filipinos have a right to a government of their own making, though we could give them a better one. Little by little the mask is being slipped aside and the cry for expansion is sounding more and more in one note. Business! Commerce! Trade! We need the islands! Our Asiatic prestige demands them! It is the clattering bills of the buzzards about the carcass. It is the selfish growl of the grizzly ripping the bowels from the huddled sheep. Are the common people themselves so blind, so deluded, or so half enslaved that they will lend themselves to the work? I ask not the greedy few, but the whole people, shall we choose profit or honor?

It is said our obligations to others demand it. I know of no obligation to others one-half as sacred as our obligation to Washington and Jefferson—our obligation to ourselves. I have been told by naval officers that the original intention was to have Dewey destroy the Spanish fleet, as a war measure, and then sail away, leaving the rest to the insurgents. Suppose this had been done, what would have been our obligation to others? The Filipinos were in rebellion and were our allies. Suppose we had handed them the fruit of the common victory, where would have been the wrong? But abandoning these radical views, what obligation of ours is it compels us to deny to the Filipinos the hope of eventually having a government of their own? What obligation compels us to declare and assume full sovereignty over these islands? By what rule of war or morals have we been compelled against our will to assume sovereignty over the Filipinos against their will?

Our former allies asked little enough of this administration as it seemed to me—only their self-government under an American advisory protectorate, and I have never yet seen the reason that compelled us to deny it and assert full sovereignty for all time over these islands. But as I shall show, this is exactly what the commission's proclamation does assert, and the modest request for a protectorate only is precisely what that proclamation denies, and though filled with soft platitudes, it holds out no hope that the request will ever be granted.

It was this determined attitude of the administration that brought on the new war with our former allies and drove Agoncillo out of Washington. Whether the expectations of the Filipinos were justified by our own words and conduct, I call a few of the facts to witness.

One year ago today the Cubans and the Filipinos were alike in rebellion against Spain. The existing insurrections were each of about three years standing. The Spanish governor at Manila reported the insurrection suppressed, but it was not true. The Cubans were near our shores, the Filipinos seven thousand miles away. The Cuban insurgents were a scattered army, carrying on a guerrilla warfare, without any city of their own, nor any sea-port, without an organized government and without funds. By land or sea they gave little real assistance to our arms. The Filipinos had no organized government. Aguinaldo had been bought off, it is said. At least he had left the country.

They also lent but little effective aid to us. So far as I can see, Cuba and Luzon stand in the same place precisely. This being the condition of affairs, our House of Representatives found its resolution of intervention. At this time the Philippines entered into no man's calculations. Why? Will any one pretend it was because we meant to give those islands different treatment from Cuba?

No! Everyone knows the Philippines were not mentioned simply because they were so far away and so far removed from the direct question. Cuba—all eyes and thoughts were on Cuba. Does anyone doubt what would have been our answer at that time if anyone had said. "How about the Philippines?" No man in his heart doubts but that, word for word, the Philippines would have been inserted alongside of Cuba, and every pledge we gave the world and Cuba would have been repeated for the Philippines. The whole trouble is that the Filipinos, worse luck for them, were so far beyond our horizon that no one thought of them.

These resolutions said that the President was authorized to intervene to stop the war in Cuba, "to the end and with the purpose of securing permanent peace and order there and establishing by the free action of the people, a stable and independent government of their own, in the island of Cuba."

The minority report was: "Resolved, That the United States Government hereby recognizes the independence of Cuba." This resolution recited that the people of Cuba have been struggling for freedom for three years (so with the Filipinos), that "their fortitude is unexcelled," that "their aspirations for liberty are noble imitations of our own example. (How about the Filipinos?)

I ask these gentlemen who are so free with the word "Copperhead," if the struggle for liberty by yellow ragged mongrels is noble in Cuba, what makes it ignoble in yellow, naked mongrels in Luzon? If the ragged, yellow Cubans were patriots imitating our own example, why is it the yellow Filipinos are "rebel niggers?" The skin is not the same, the costume is not the same, the time and place are not the same, but it seems to me the principle is the same in Luzon today, as in Philadelphia, July 4, 1776.

In the Senate, the majority report directed the President to intervene to end the war, and to direct Spain to withdraw from the island. The minority report was, as in the House, a recognition of Cuban independence. Speaking to the majority report, Senator Lodge said: "What kind of government can alone observe international obligations? Only an independent government." The air of both chambers vibrated to the cry of "a holy war," "war for humanity," "a war to rescue the oppressed," "a war with no thought of self or gain," etc., and this same Senator Lodge said war could never come in a holier cause. April 19—a year ago next Tuesday, the House and Senate passed this joint resolution:

Joint resolution for the recognition of the independence of the people of Cuba, demanding that the government of Spain relinquish its authority and government in the island of Cuba, and to withdraw its land and naval forces from

Cuba and Cuban waters, and directing the President of the United States to use the land and naval forces of the United States to carry this resolution into effect.

Whereas. The abhorrent conditions which have existed for more than three years in the island of Cuba, so near our own borders, have shocked the moral sense of the people of the United States, have been a disgrace to Christian civilization, culminating, as they have, in the destruction of a United States battle-ship and 266 of its officers and crew, while on a friendly visit in the harbor of Havana, cannot be longer endured, as has been set forth by the President of the United States in his message to congress[42] of April 11, 1898, upon which the action of congress was invited; therefore, be it Resolved, By the senate and house of representatives of the United States of America, in congress assembled:

First—That the people of the island of Cuba, are, and of right ought to be, free and independent.

Second—That it is the duty of the United States to demand, and the government of the United States does hereby demand, that the government of Spain at once relinquish its authority and government in the island of Cuba, and withdraw its land and naval forces from Cuba and Cuban waters.

Third—That the President of the United States be, and is hereby directed and empowered to use the entire land and naval forces of the United States, and to call into the actual service of the United States the militia of the several states to

---

[42] This quotation did not capitalize Congress, House or Senate and this original spelling has been retained.

such extent as may be necessary to carry these resolutions into effect.

Fourth—That the United States hereby disclaims any disposition to exercise sovereignty, jurisdiction or control over said island, except for the pacification thereof; and asserts its determination, when that is accomplished, to leave the government and control of the island to its people.

In the light of all the circumstances, I ask you, my friends. I ask this honest nation, if the Filipinos reading these speeches and this resolution would not have been justified in hugging themselves with joy in the belief that what was said of the Cubans was meant also for the Filipinos.

If there was no reason to exercise sovereignty over Cuba, whose shores were in sight of our shores, would not the Filipinos believe there was even less reason for any claim of sovereignty over an island seven thousand miles away. If it was a war of humanity to end Spanish oppression and misrule, and to establish a free and independent government in Cuba, what law of humanity is it that turns the same war into one of conquest and enforced government in Luzon?

Had the Filipinos been but a hundred miles from our shores what would they have thought of our words? What would they have had a right to think of our words? Would it have occurred to them that this unselfish war for humanity was founded in hair splitting? Would they not have had a right to say, "True, the resolution says only Cuba, but the splendid spirit of that unselfish and Christian resolution floats out to us. Cannot every word that is said of Cuba, be said equally of us?" But if some common Shylock had said, "Only Cuba is nominated in the bond," would not the Filipinos have been justified in saying, "Out upon thee, thou buyer of human flesh! Our name is omitted only because we were not thought of. We are within the spirit of the law."

And now, to our very shame, this argument rises from the administration leaders, from this same Senator Lodge, "Luzon was nominated in the bond." And with the snivel of the pettifogger, we swear our justice to Cuba with our lies to Luzon. Let me repeat again, till they echo outside of this room, the words that began this war. "This is a war for humanity. This is not a war for conquest or selfish gain." This is our pledge to Cuba, and through Cuba, to Christendom. How many miles, then, of ocean does it take to drown the honor of the young republic? I hope to God the plain common people, the soul of this nation, will take from the wily politicians the jewel they have tarnished. I hope and pray to God that not all the fathoms of blue water on the globe will wash out the solemn vow of the American people. And I hope to God that infamy will be the lot of those entrusted with the faith of the nation who have broken that faith and juggled with the letter of its promise.

April the 20th, the President signed this joint resolution. It was conveyed to Spain as an ultimatum, and on April 25th war was declared. President McKinley, in both his messages, had said (1897-1898): "Sure of the right. Keeping free from all offense ourselves, actuated by upright and patriotic considerations, moved neither by passions nor selfishness," etc., etc. But the smoke of Dewey's guns had scarcely blown out of Manila Bay, when Senator Lodge and the President's other advisers made haste to say (May 6th), that the Philippines must be held permanently, "because the United States had long desired to increase her Oriental prestige." Thus the platitudes of our worthy President, "sure of the right," "moved not by selfishness," became less enduring than the smoke of the guns.

In both of his messages, the President said: "I speak not of forcible annexation, for that cannot be thought of; that by our code of morality would be criminal aggression." Criminal aggression! Those are the words for Cuba, but in the travel over seven thousand miles of sea to Luzon, they change to the canting whine of "benevolent assimilation." Criminal aggression under our code of morality becomes under the lights and through the wine of the Home Market Club, benevolent assimilation.

When Major McKinley is answering to the conscience of the American people he says to annex the people against their will, even though they be at our doors, would be criminal aggression, but when he is answering to the wealth and greed and desires of the Home Market Club, he finds the same forcible annexation of a far, distant people, is "benevolent assimilation."

I respect the office of the President of the United States. It shall have my loyalty and my support. I have tried to consider the trials and responsibilities of that office, but it seems to me courageous manliness should be as easy to a President as to a citizen, and no man, as a man, can have my personal respect, who gives over his army to politics, surrenders his self declared code of national morality to selfish interest, and has no higher aspiration or truer guide than the next national convention. As he was silver, so he became gold. As he is now a benevolent assimilator by criminal aggression, or a criminal aggressor by benevolent assimilation, so he will, if the signs of the times demand it, abandon his present attitude and explain with fat, smelling platitudes, the ditches filled with dead Filipinos and the American hearths desolate in a war against weak and confiding allies.

May 9th, 1898, Dewey suggests a plan of a provisional government. May 14th he reports a strict blockade and says the rebels are hemming Manila by land. In view of our present condition, I ought to say "rebels" meant then rebels against Spain. Alexandrino, one of Aguinaldo's lieutenants, had come over on Dewey's ship. Aguinaldo was in Hong Kong, arranging for funds and for a native government under an American protectorate. All that they ever asked was their own government under an American protectorate. It was all Agoncillo asked at Washington. They only asked what we are giving Cuba. I ought to say my facts are largely from newspaper clippings, but I have not seen them contradicted.

Dewey announced also that the insurgent policy was an independent government, under an American protectorate. The insurgents loaded a ship with arms and ammunition, and safely landed the cargo, May 4. It was reported Aguinaldo had arrived and would co-operate with Dewey. It is claimed by some that the insurgents gave Dewey valuable information concerning the harbor; that they hemmed in Manila from the rear and rendered much service. I care not whether they did or did not. I can only see that they, like the Cubans, were insurgents. They, like the Cubans, were our allies. They, like the Cubans, desired an independent government under American protection and advice. They, unlike the Cubans, were bought from the very government they helped subdue, and instead of even a government under an American protectorate, they get pitiless death. Benevolent assimilation! Aye, in truth, this is benevolent assimilation, for dead in trenches the Filipino knows neither war, nor oppression, and his heart ceases to long for the right to live in his own poor way.

Our President points to the flag that was borne to the relief of these struggling Filipinos, and asks who would take it down. Let me answer; if I found I had another's goods, I would not be ashamed to restore them. If I had lied to a man, I would be ashamed to own it, but I would be a better man if I did so, and I say to the administration, you have placed the first great blot on the Stars and Stripes with your duplicity, your timidity, your thirst for power and gain, and I for one, will never forgive you—never! never! never! Better haul down the flag ourselves in honor than keep it there in deliberate dishonor.

I cannot respect a man whose code of morality makes forcible annexation in Cuba benevolent assimilation in Luzon. I cannot respect a logic which admits the yellow mongrels of Cuba to be fitted for independence under an American protectorate, and denies the same thing to the yellow mongrels of Luzon. The ambassadors they have sent, their conduct in the warfare now going on, the men who compose their juntas and so-called Congress show them in better light than the Cubans. I have been told by officers of Dewey's fleet and others that the leaders are men educated in Paris and London; that nearly all the common people read and write; that pianos and pictures are common in even humble houses; that a ball given by the insurgents was made up of ladies and gentlemen of education and refinement, dressed in full Parisian style.

It is pitiful to me to read of the poor peasant, coming with his bow and arrows, his blow-gun, his spear, his knife, or some old weapon to fight the desperate fight against the new conqueror. It is more pitiful to me to read now and again of the death of some splendid young son of the nation in such a war. We were solemnly pledged in this war to gain no new territory, to annex forcibly no people, to conquer only in honor. That pledge was as true, aye, truer in Luzon than in Cuba, and I cannot forgive the administration that out of the contest for honor, has brought us only dishonor.

When we paid the twenty millions and claimed the purchase of a people against their will, we did a dishonorable act. I shall not palter with the human spiders who spin the web of constitutional and international law. I care not if Spain had or had not the goods to deliver. This is a question of flesh and blood, not cobwebs, and though we might pay the twenty millions as an end to peace, every honest man will rub his

84

palm with disgust at the thought that our dirty dollars bought a people and gave us a right to war against them.

I say we cannot in honor give the Filipinos a lighter yoke for a heavier, a better master for a worse against their will. I say if it was a war for our allies in Cuba, it was a war for our allies in the Philippines. We are committed to establish an independent government in Cuba and retire. What do we offer the Filipinos? Read the proclamation. Through all the smooth phrases and McKinley platitudes is the clear statement that the United States asserts and will maintain sovereignty. Not till the purchase of this sovereignty, not till the determination to hold the islands for ourselves was declared, did the prayers to us for decency and mercy cease, and our late honorable allies become rebels and "niggers." The proclamation says among other things, "The aim and object of the American government, apart from the fulfillment of the solemn obligations it has assumed toward the family of nations in the acceptance of sovereignty over the Philippines, etc. * * *."

They (the Filipinos) are patriots and want liberty, it is said. The Commission emphatically asserts that the United States is not only willing, but anxious to establish in the Philippine Islands an enlightened system of government, under which the Philippine people can enjoy the largest measure of home rule, "consonant with the supreme end of the government, etc. * * *" "There can be no real conflict between the American sovereignty and the rights and liberties of the Philippine people, for as the United States stand ready to furnish armies and navies, and the infinite resources of a great and powerful nation to maintain and support its rightful supremacy over the Philippine Islands, etc."

It is pretty clear our yellow allies in the Pacific are getting different measure from our yellow allies in the Atlantic, and that "conquest," "selfishness," "forcible annexation," "criminal aggression," "national code of morality," all depend on geographical location.

What they may really hope for is as vague as a plank in a McKinley platform. This American sovereignty is to guarantee the Filipinos, "their rightful freedom, protect them in their just privileges and immunities, accustom them to free self-government in ever increasing measure (sounds like a diet regulation), encourage them in those democratic aspirations, sentiments and ideals which are the promise of potency and fruitful of national development."

I can imagine the Filipino small farmer gathering his half-naked family about him in the evening and reading to them this precious promise of McKinley potency. The English language is richer for that proclamation, and it is a wonder to me Mr. Dooley has not discussed it. The English language is richer for it, and American national honor is damned. But before the mysterious obligations to the family of nations have to be met, before the armies and navies of a nation of infinite resources that has a labor strike every month and a higher average of crime than any civilized nation on earth, are called out, the American people will have to be reckoned with. The armies and navies and infinite resources of the limited states are not yet wholly at the beck and call of Mr. McKinley, Messrs. Hanna, Alger, Brother Abner and the Home Market Club.

Gentlemen, nearly a quarter of a century[43] ago, he whose birth we commemorate, wrote: "We hold these truths to be self-evident, that all men are created equal. That they are endowed by their Creator with certain unalienable rights, that among these are life, liberty, and the pursuit of happiness. That to secure these rights governments are instituted among men, deriving their just powers from the consent of the governed." This was our baptismal gift. This the very core and essence of our beginning. Only one element in all our young life gave these words the lie, and that blot was wiped clean with the blood of sacrifice, and those letters have stood forth from that day as letters of gold upon a shield of silver.

Are those words true, or are they not true?? Is it time, or is it not time, gentlemen, that men have a right to life, liberty and happiness; to pursue their own life in their own way, and to have some voice in the law to which they yield obedience? Is it true, or is it not true? If it be true, then the savage has an unalienable right to live in a palm thatched hut and eat raw fish if he finds there greater happiness, rather than be well housed and fed in the rice fields of the tax gatherer.

If it be true at all it is as true for the poor Filipino in 1899 as it was for the enlightened American in 1776. His soil is his

---

[43] This should be read "a century and a quarter ago" in order to make sense. It may have been an error in the speech or, more likely, a transcription error.

soil, and we cannot by force of conquest or barter of gold enslave a nation, unless we have put behind us once and forever the Declaration of Independence. It was not a declaration for ourselves alone. It was a mighty trumpet from the vast heights of freedom, proclaiming to the poor and oppressed of all the earth, "Throw off your chains, ye wretched ones; ye have the God-given right to rule yourselves." It was not the voice of Jefferson or the fathers. It was the voice of the God in man, and though we strangle liberty in her chosen temple, she will not die, nor that voice be silent. More than a century before Jefferson, Oliver Cromwell wrote on the statute book of Parliament: "All just powers under God are derived from the people." Cromwell's ashes were scattered to the winds and the harlots of Charles' Court danced over his silent grave. But they have passed and still lives this truth— all just powers under God come from the people.

We may forget honor in trade; we may indeed be tools in the hands of the covetous; we may sing soothing songs to ourselves that we are buying a people for their own good, enslaving a people for their own benefit, but the old, old lie will not live, and though our great cities become as the desert places of the earth and in the harbors of New York and San Francisco there shall be nowhere seen the stars and stripes; though we have passed away and sleep with Babylon and Rome, still will live the truth, and the historian will write upon our ruins, "They are dead because in the drunkenness of their power they belied themselves and denied that governments derive their just powers from the consent of the governed."

Oh, gentlemen, I am so far human that I cannot desert my flag and my countrymen. I cannot take from my heart the sympathies I have for men of my own blood and the glorious banner I have served. But were I a Filipino and thought upon my long struggle against the Spaniard, the dawn of hope in my breast as I watched coming from the East across the sea, the strong, Young Giant of the West, the bitterness to find he came with hammer and sword, not to strike off my shackles, but to rivet them faster, I would in my despair put my young ones and their mother in the cane, and I would fight, fight, fight till the sun was blotted from my eyes.

The Manhattan Club Speech[44]

Delivered February 22, 1902

This commentary and partial reproduction of the speech is the most complete that the editor found. It is possible that the full text exists in Wood's papers.

But the one vital, full-blooded and inspiring speech of the evening came at the close. Inspiring as it was, however, it spread consternation among the little chieftains who had worked up this boom for Hill.[45] That one soul-stirring and "heeler"-crushing speech is worthy of special consideration.

At the guest table sat a stranger of singular personal appearance, who had been noticed by some of the curious. His head covered with

---

[44] Excerpts as reported in *The Public* magazine, Vol 4, p. 734-735 (March, 1902).

[45] Former New York Governor David Hill was attempting to generate a campaign for the presidency rooted in the idea of reorganizing the party around a pro-business platform and leaving out the Bryanite focus on rural interests and free silver. The party eventually nominated a conservative judge, Alton Parker from New York, which had the effect of alienating many natural Democratic voters without attracting business people suspicious of the party's history, which resulted in the election of Theodore Roosevelt to a full term in 1904. Parker did not carry a single state outside the South.

clustering curls, and on his breast a frilled shirt bosom supported by a white waistcoat the cut of which would have defied description, he might have taken the grand prize at a nineteenth century fashion show. He was evidently a man of means, accustomed to refined society, and, as his speech proved, he had command of a cultured and effective style of oratory. But while he sat at the guest table during the dinner he looked like some rare human exotic.

Had he not spoken, his striking personality might have been remembered with an impression that he was probably a French poet or an Oriental prince traveling incognito. In fact, he is well known upon the Pacific coast as C. E. S. Wood, a lawyer of large practice and extraordinary ability, whose home is Portland, and who is a democratic-Democrat and that to the core. When introduced as a speaker at the Manhattan banquet, his voice rang out clear, strong, masculine and honest; and he flew at his subject like a hawk to the prey.

At first the whole audience was enthusiastic, but as he unfolded the democratic principles of the Pacific coast, for which he spoke, one part of his audience was aghast, though the rest were delighted.

Mr. Wood said in substance that he came from the West, where men's minds were influenced by their environments—by the vast prairies, the deep mines, the extensive ranches and the mountains that reach the sky. These surroundings caused men, he said, to look things in the face and have an independent democratic spirit that allowed the theaters and the saloons as well as the churches to be wide open on Sunday, and that gave every man the privilege of going to Tophet if he wanted to.

It was this feeling of independence, he proceeded, that impelled him to look about and ask himself with whom he was to "get together"' for 1904, and he confessed that the prospect was not good. It indicated that he might have to "get together" with himself, for, said he: "I voted for McKinley in 1896; for Bryan in 1900; and now, I do not see 'that there is any kind of a real Democratic party for me to act with.'

The audience hesitated. It had laughed loudly at the allusion to the saloons, and it had learned that Wood was a fine speaker with strong views, but it wondered what he could say, after that declaration, under the head, of Democratic "harmony." The speaker went on:

> We talk of uniting the elements of the party. What is a party? What is the Democratic party? If it is anything it must be a gathering around a principle, around a great idea. But what are we talking of? Gathering the elements; getting together the parts of the party. What are the parts and what are the elements? The party cannot have more than one element, nor more than one part, if it is democratic. The plain truth we should face; and we should honestly tell ourselves that what we are trying to do is to get into or hold inside the Democratic party a lot of people who are not democrats and who should not be in the party. The best way for us to start in to "get together" is to put out these men who don't belong here. Then, when those who remain are of one mind, they can preach their democratic faith and make recruits.

At that, the plutocrats in the audience gasped, and the faces of some were like untinted wax. This harmony movement for Hill was fast losing its way. But Wood was merciless. With unmistakable allusions to Hill's keynote speech he went on:

It has been said that tariff reform is a good issue for the party. But is it? Suppose some of the Democrats in the North and West want free trade in sugar, what will the Louisiana senators and congressmen do about it? Will they submit? I don't think so. And so you may go through the list of the tariff schedules. Then we are told that regulations of the trusts is a good Democratic issue. Is it? Regulate them how? By law. But have we ever regulated the railroads by law, or the Standard Oil company by law? Let me say that we never, never can regulate anything by law that has its roots deep down in existing social conditions. Those things are too strong to be regulated by law. The truth is that these are not the real Democratic issues and cannot be. They are but changing phases of the ever present issue for Democracy. That issue is "privilege." Look at the great fortunes of to-day. Are they made by ability? The great mass of men have difficulty to keep body and soul together, and some other men have unthinkable fortunes. Can we say that the mental powers of the few are as superior to those of the many as the riches of those few are in contrast, with the poverty of the many? I don't believe it. It is not natural. I don't want to say anything against riches. What I want to say is that the masses of the people are not getting their rights. And it is the Democratic party's business to get them their rights—to make war upon privilege, which is depriving them of their rights.

An assault upon privilege, so unrestrained and manifestly so sincere, touched several individuals in the audience, and they applauded: but the same manifest sincerity which appealed to them, froze to the marrow the plutocrats who were accustomed to refer as tenderly to privilege as did Hill, when in his speech he guardedly mentioned the "dangerous, corporate combinations of capital." But Wood was not through. Heeding neither cheers nor scowls he drove on to his mark:

Perhaps this is not the view of Democracy here. But I want to say that I have been called to speak for the West coast; and my say is that the pressing, palpitating thought among the great mass of men there is that somewhere, somehow, there is a great wrong that causes some men to have a superabundance and other men not enough to live good lives, though they work with all their might. And I want to say that this thought is going down to the foundations. It is going down to the roots. Men are asking themselves why it is that some few human beings are accorded the right to keep all others from the use of the land; why it is that persons who call themselves owners are permitted to lay claim and keep idle great stretches of country while other men are forced to compete with each other for a living? It is not right. Anybody who thinks about it can see that it is not right, and I want to say to this meeting of Democrats that the real principle of Democracy has sooner or later got to take up that, question and settle it on the principle of equal rights, notwithstanding titles and parchments.

No wonder that reports of this speech were suppressed. Had it gone into the papers it would have been as crushing a climax to the absurd Hill boom throughout the country as it was in the banquet hall, where it turned the boom into a boomerang, simply by sharply contrasting democratic Democracy with plutocratic Democracy. This was a true contrast and no mere sentiment. Wood represented the anti-monopoly spirit of the Western farms and ranches, which will rule the Democratic convention of 1904 as certainly as it did the conventions of 1896 and 1900, and which would no sooner tolerate Hill as its presidential candidate now than then, or than it would tolerate J. Pierpont Morgan or Perry Belmont. ...[46]

---

[46] Roosevelt's attempt to win as an independent on the Progressive Party ticket in 1912 did not succeed, but in that campaign he made his own views on the role of government in the preservation of freedom clear in a San Francisco speech:

"So long as governmental power existed exclusively for the king and not at all for the people, then the history of liberty was a history of the limitation of governmental power. But now the governmental power rests in the people, and the kings who enjoy privilege are the kings of the financial and industrial world; and what they clamor for is the

Transmutation of Virtues into Vices

The Pacific Monthly 20, no. 4 (October 1908): 454-455.[47]

I believe a very tolerable essay could be written on the transmutation of virtues into vices—perhaps it has been done. There is no new thing under the sun—a saying I give little adherence to. Proverbs, maxims and such generalizations would find the lie every day, if it were looked for. There is much new under the sun—and it is not impossible that some day an  editor may have a principle, and a great daily tell the truth. This old world is ever new—that is the fascination of it. Not only new to each of us who opens his eyes for the first time upon the panorama and frets across the stage his brief moment—but in truth new—new lands, new life, new thoughts. And there is the very core of the matter—new thoughts.

---

limitation of governmental power, and what the people sorely need is the extension of governmental power."

If modern-day Libertarians want to reduce the frequency of such Theodorian attitudes today, they would do well to note the underlying rationale for the 1912 speech.

[47] Bust of Wood by Olin Levi Warner from the Portland Public Library.

People talk of unchanging human nature—eternally the same. Human nature is changing as much as the human body did and probably much more and faster than the human body is now changing, though it is dangerous to speculate on evolution in which millions of years are minutes. The body has adapted itself to its present environment, and little change may be expected unless the environment changes; but the environment of mind and thought is constantly changing before our very eyes, and human nature is changing with it.

Does anyone fancy that we have the human nature of the cave dwellers? Gentlemen whose conception of justice was appetite and the might to gratify it; who did not on occasion hesitate to eke out the scant subsistence of a non-prosperous administration by devouring their grandmothers and other weak antiques; and quite right, too, from the view point of nature. We ourselves must admit that we would rather have the cave dwelling paterfamilias and his amiable mate preserve the divine spark for transmission to us, by recourse to grandpa or grandma as a larder rather than that by self-denial and literal self-sacrifice, all human life should become extinct and we ourselves be barred from our succession to this wonderful world of nickel-in-the-slot drama and tinhorn tragedy.

There is no doubt that, as we picture the cave gentleman at his necessitous or perhaps diplomatic meal with bloody front gnawing the raw bones of his mother-in-law—nephew, grandfather, or whichever relative his taste and an overruling providence decreed should be removed from their midst to his; we realize that we of to-day have progressed in our nature; even an editor has a somewhat different cannibalistic method, and presumably a different nature.

But those who cling to the absolute unchanging quality of human nature will say: Take an editor, even the greatest, and put him on a raft in mid-ocean—the reader will understand that this is wholly hypothetical God forbid that any editor, even the greatest, should in fact be put on a raft in mid-ocean and the world left rocking in chaos—take an editor, the objector will say (as if the editor were a worm,) and put him on a raft in mid-ocean with one other and no food and he will devour his companion as relishfully as did our late lamented ancestor of the cave.

The world is full of the self-sacrifice of the strong for the weak. Common sailors have said good-bye to a comrade and let go the support too frail for both.

It was Greenwood, I think, who shut himself in the leaking air-lock of the Hudson river tunnel to drown rather than drown the four or five laborers he had put through to safety. It is a pity to forget the names of such heroes— greater than those of war—but after all the name is not so material; the important fact is that human nature furnishes such examples—many of them. Cave-dwelling human nature furnished not one.

The cave gentleman's effort at charity was doubtless to crush the skull of the sufferer with a stone—a method having certainly some advantages over ours, but as a whole we have progressed in conception and intention.

But we need not harry too cruelly the shades of our cave ancestors who lived the truly simple life. The historic ancients of the really splendid civilizations of Greece and Rome did not have the emotions of pity for humanity and dumb brutes as we have them, nor the sense of duty toward the unfortunate as we have it. Nay, there are whole nations to-day who have not developed into their natures the sense of brotherhood of man and kinship with animals. 'Where we find but so much as one example of a new trait in human nature, that gives us a right to claim it to our credit.

It is perfectly true that the evolution of a finer human nature or soul builds upon fundamentals. While the desire to live is a general human instinct, there will be the desire to eat and enjoy life, out of which must come the struggle for comfort and joy, and from this struggle, of necessity, selfishness. Selfishness is the most desirable thing in the world. It is the electrifying spark, the vital emotion. It is a virtue and yet behold how the virtue of the cave-dweller, when the great essential was that life should not vanish from the planet and that the fittest should survive, becomes the vice of our time when the mentally predatory and by no means fittest are crushing those who, because of loftier ideals or simpler honesty are open to exploitation.

Altruism, or thought for others, self-sacrifice, unselfishness has been developed by the Christian impulse into the chiefest of the virtues. If you have not this then are you but as sounding brass or tinkling cymbal.

Yet what a vice this virtue may become. How many unselfish wives do we see being devoured by selfish husbands, or husbands by wives; patient daughters wearing out their lives in subjection to demanding mothers. Lives of men and women literally sucked dry by good, virtuous, loving, selfish vampires. When what every life craves is freedom—free, free to live its own life in its own way, giving expression to all which bubbles up from within.

It matters nothing at all if there be a heaven where the selfish will be punished and the unselfish rewarded. Let heaven take care of itself. No one has a right to ask another to give up his individuality in this world, to lose his quota of present joy and trust to a heavenly reward. It is not a fair bargain.

I do not say to the leeches: Be less selfish. Do not suck dry these lives about you. It would be a useless appeal, for such is their nature; but I do say to the victims (in some hope that I may be heard because of the fundamental instinct of selfishness within us all): Be more selfish—your life was given to you to live. Live it. Draw the line between a just attention to others and your essential duty to yourself. Let living be reciprocal. Let the parasites upon you also give. If all cannot be unselfish, then let all be selfish.[48]

---

[48] Wood's unusual appeal to selfishness, written in 1908, presages Ayn Rand's essay collection *The Virtue of Selfishness* (1964), the title of which she considered intentionally provocative.

The word has got an ugly meaning—people pretend to recoil from the trait it expresses—none recoil more than those very ones who are sucking the lives of others. My own irritation is not so much with the selfish ones who rule, who master, who override, who demand, who receive and who absorb—they are at least following their natures—as with the unselfish ones who do not oppose to this selfishness an equal selfishness; who stifle because of what I think is a false ideal, the natural desire to live their own lives. I do not believe they are following their natures so much as their ideals of duty. Whatever may come hereafter, this world is all we know. It stands upon its own footing, and no person has a right to absorb the life of another, and no person has a right to let his individuality and his life-expression and life-longings be absorbed by another. His highest duty, higher than any other possible, for it is to the race as well as to himself, is to live his own life in his own way to the very fullness thereof.

The virtues as well as the vices have their root in selfishness. It is the parent stock; and what are virtues and what are vices will always be open to dispute. Pride is a virtue as self-respect; it is a vice as exaggerated self-esteem. Love may be a vice and hate a virtue, so these names go masquerading under different guises, according to the motive, the object and the degree.

Of the primal instincts—offshoots from selfishness—jealousy is the one which I cannot find virtuous in any degree. In the form of parental solicitude it may be accepted, but the variety which we have developed in the sex relation is wholly bad. It is brutal and unintellectual, prolific of much misery, narrowing to life and debasing to the soul. I have heard people actually defend jealousy by saying it is common to the brutes, that the dog, the cat, the horse show jealousy. Curious recommendation.

I have no doubt the late lamented cave-dweller, in his impulse to sex supremacy, slaughtered his rivals precisely as one Captain Hains has recently done, [49] though the gallant Captain is additionally the victim of an artificial development called "Honor." The sense of ownership of his mate in the savage can be understood, especially as he bought her—but just how a man's honor is blotted by any act of another of which he had no knowledge, I cannot comprehend. My honor is in my own keeping; and to my way of thinking an unfaithful wife can be left to her choice with greater honor than to commit murder for her sake.

I write these impressions too hurriedly ever to be thorough (and by the way they are in no sense the editorials of this magazine, but my personal impressions for what they may be worth). What I intend to offer as food for better and deeper thought than mine is that selfishness, self-interest, measurement by the scale of self, self-gratification is the root of all impulses and human attributes, and unless we are to believe Nature (or God) all wrong, we cannot believe selfishness to be wrong. That in fact the same trait may be a

---

[49] This is presumably a reference to the August, 1908 murder of a rival (alleged to be sleeping with his wife) by Captain Thornton Hains and his brother. It received heavy news coverage at the time.

virtue or a vice according to the circumstances of application, and that it is by no means a virtue to crush out ourselves idolatrously before the unchecked selfishness of another or others—rather it is the highest duty to live our lives according to the deep longings thereof—for the longings are of God and no man can say what great good may come to the world from their full and free expression.

The world is full of idols; we bow down to them and worship them, and though they are senseless images, we ourselves are not so, and it is by our own conceptions which we accept as coming from the idol that we enslave ourselves. Let our conceptions therefore be Just. Measure them more by ourselves and our rights to life and in life, and we will find that much which we have called duty, honor, obedience, self-sacrifice, are fetishes, and the whole world will be juster and saner and happier—I truly believe far, far happier when they are overthrown.

On Privilege

The following segment is one of Wood's most detailed discussions of privilege in society, from his "Impressions" column in *Pacific Monthly*. Part 1 of the three-part discussion appeared in Vol. 25, pages 328-332 (March, 1911). Part 2 appeared on pages 440-444 (April, 1911) and Part 3 on pages 556-564 (May, 1911). They are combined here and have been given the collective title "On Privilege" by the current author, not by Wood.[50]

Part 1

March 1911

It is said of the Direct Primary that by removing the guiding hands of the "Leaders" it permits a free-for-all race, in which mediocre men are apt to be successful: but could it possibly be worse than the purchase of a seat in the United States Senate, or than the hand of a Murphy, guiding the star of Sheehan—and distinctly repudiating Edward M. Shepard? The ground

---

[50] Photo: Charles Erskine Scott Wood, 1910, from *History of the Bench and Bar of Oregon.* Portland, Or: Historical Pub. Co.

for opposing Mr. Shepard is that he is a corporation lawyer. He is. One of the best in the country—and well were it for country and corporations if all corporation counsel were like him. A man of unswerving integrity, of inbred sympathy with the people, a true Democrat by instinct, he guides his corporations—not they him. But think of the objection from a Murphy and a Sheehan that he is a corporation lawyer! The trouble is, neither corporations nor Mr. Murphy could control Mr. Shepard; but Mr. Sheehan would be one more agent in the House of Privileges. The objection to Mr. Shepard, coming whence it does and taking the form it does, is farce-tragedy.

Mr. Shepard was of the firm of Parsons, Shepard and Ogden, which organized the sugar trust, Mr. Parsons being the active attorney, and no suggestion has ever been made that it was an unlawful act, and not a breath of scandal or suspicion of impropriety attaches to Mr. Shepard. In all his active political life—as Democratic candidate for Mayor of Greater New York in 1901— never has his perfect integrity been questioned. Everywhere his name has stood and stands for the highest type of Democrat, lawyer and citizen. But more than that, he believes that the supreme test is the welfare of the people, and as general counsel for the Pennsylvania Railroad he has been instrumental in creating a corporate feeling and policy, that the great public service corporations are in fact only trustees for and servants of the Public—and the Public is to be taken into the corporate confidence. The result has been that the Pennsylvania is today strong in the good will of the people.

Is a man to be blindly attacked merely because he has been the legal adviser of corporations, without regard to how he has advised them? Must the man who has stood firm for corporate righteousness be insanely classed with the man who has helped to corporate plunderings? Blind as the plain people are, they are not so blind as that. There is none so blind as a Tammany Boss who will not see.

Mr. Shepard is peculiarly equipped for the position of United States Senator. A student of history and of political science; author of a work on the period of Martin Van Buren; opposed to protection and jingoism; opposed to Special Privileges, he would, as a lawmaker, restrict them. A Democrat in the true sense that he believes in the plain people; one of the most eminent lawyers in the United States; a man entitled to be called a statesman, who would quickly and easily lead in a greater body than the United States Senate, and all this thrown away by the State of New York because Shepard doesn't suit the dirty ambitions of Boss Murphy! Could the people at the Direct Primary, or by the Popular Election of Senators, do worse? Turn where you will, the truth becomes larger and clearer that, as Governor Woodrow Wilson says, the old era of machine politics has reached its full rottenness, and some new system must be tried with greater hope for a true execution of the people's will— a government by the people, for the people.

It would be well if all controllers of corporations could take to heart one of the maxims of Mr. Shepard. "A corporation which serves the public and depends on the public for its profits, can have no greater asset than the affection and trust of the people it serves. ... This affection and trust can be gained not by log-rolling and lobbying, not by forms of respectable filching and selfish depredation, but by absolute honesty, open frankness having nothing to be ashamed of, by making the public a partner in your confidence and seeking only the just reward which no fair man would deny. Knowing all the facts."

Compare such a creed with the school of Get All You Can And How You Can—by control of the lawmaking powers, and executive powers by lobbies, and briberies more or less direct— a curious code of morals which if applied between man and man in the matter of a horse or a farm, would be called lying and cheating and stealing.

The business management of this magazine has been warned that unless the magazine ceases to be so "anti-corporation" and "radical" it must expect to lose a large part of its advertising—I am the offender. I am sorry for this. I am sorry for myself, for I hate to give offense, yet there are times when not to offend is unrighteous. I am sorry for the business management, for it has a hard problem: to maintain a readable magazine[51] with some character to it and yet which will please everybody and more, too. I don't know any one who subsists on all kicks except the business management of a magazine. No one extends the glad hand of encouragement, but the foot is ever ready. After all, what profiteth it a magazine that it gain a whole world of advertising and lose its

---

[51] Typographical error in original corrected.

own soul? (Read William Winter's article in the last number on the subserviency of the newspapers to the great advertisers.)

Most of all, I am sorry for the people who are offended, because it must be that to them a free expression of opinion is distasteful. Now the way I look at it is that discussion can harm nothing which is just. If the views are not somewhere rooted in truth they are bound to fail—just as certainly as the raindrops fall. And if they do hang upon even the edges of Truth, in God's name let us have them as quickly, as widely, as we can.

Speaking for a clearer understanding of terms, I have never attacked corporations as such. The corporation is a most useful form of social economic organization, and should have all the rights of the individual, so far as they are necessary to its purposes. What I have attacked are Special Privileges. They are quite as unjust and evil if vested in a man as if enjoyed by a corporation—except that the corporation is more impersonal, and more enduring, than a man, and therefore a more dangerous repository for Privilege. That most Privileges are availed of by men organized as corporations is immaterial. It is the Privilege which is dangerous, not the corporation. Special Privileges are as unjust vested in kings and an aristocracy as in self-made magnates and a plutocracy. The whole question is, how much is a man really achieving in a free environment, or how much is he sequestrating by Special Privileges? The former is his own, the latter is legalized robbery of others. I am sorry this question has come up, for I did want to write about the weather.

This is the 27th of January, a lovely spring day, and four days ago 1 heard a song sparrow making the world musical from a spirea bush, which was timidly pricking its buds into points of green—the pussy willows hang silvern tassels abundantly in the lowlands. The skies are wonderful in their delicate grey, and soft, slowly voyaging masses—through which sometimes comes a patch of blue or a golden glow. All this beauty of a divine world calls me more than the ignorance and injustice of man. Certainly I would rather write about the weather, but I must make my defense, and I choose the method of the great apologist, Socrates. I will seek to prove that those who criticise must either say just what I do, or they do not believe what they profess.

✦

Socrates: What are you two discussing so angrily?

Demos: Pluto here says I ought to be ashamed of myself to agitate the people and arouse discontent and set class against class.

Socrates: Do you indeed do this?

Pluto: Indeed he does. He tells the common people they are being robbed by the rich, who have by their riches secured control of the government, and then by the government have created Special Privileges to increase their riches. So he tears down confidence and destroys the machinery of the social order, and chaos will ensue.

Socrates: I did not suppose Demos was so wicked a man. What have you to say to this Demos?

Demos: I say, Socrates, that it seems to me like this: There is but one source of all property, commodities and wealth whatever—the earth—and but one instrument for wresting from the earth-mother all possible forms of necessities, luxuries and wealth whatever—Man's Labor.

Socrates: Wait a minute. Do you include in the word labor, man's mental labor and ingenuity of brain?

Demos: Certainly I do.

Socrates: Well, then, you mean to say man's labor creates from the earth all the property of man. Is that it?

Demos: That is it.

Socrates: Well, go on.

Demos: Now the social or organized state is like a hive of bees, where the workers (by which I mean brain workers as well as hand workers) create all the honey, but as fast as they bring it in to the hive an acquisitive few, armed with special powers given by the state, take from all the workers all the honey save only just enough for them to continue to labor on. And these lords of the hive pile up their accumulations, which become vaster as the workers become more numerous or the fields more abundant with nectar, and if any of the workers fall sick or are starving, the acquisitive lords give them a little out of their abundance, calling it charity, and the sick or hungry workers are very grateful for receiving back a part of their own earnings—but if some grumble, then the acquisitive lords show the instruments by which they extract all the honey, and say: "You see these are created by law, therefore, what we take is lawfully ours. You are agitators, who seek to overthrow society."

Pluto: That IS a very long speech, with very little sense. Men are not bees—and besides, bees have a queen and aristocratic drones.

Demos: Yes, the queen is the mother of the entire hive, and all its colonies, and does more labor than any one; and the drones, they kill. But yes, bees are not men. It was only an illustration.

Socrates: It is not clear to me yet what you two are quarreling about. Is it that it is wrong to agitate or to discuss—or that the ideas Demos is promulgating are evil and untrue?

Pluto: It is the latter, Socrates.

Socrates: Then you do not claim it is wrong to agitate and discuss new ideas?

Pluto: Not if they are sound and true ideas.

Socrates: But how are we to recognize the true from the untrue?

Pluto: Oh—by their inherent quality, their natural merit.

Socrates: But we are talking of ideas, Pluto. Ideas do not come branded like loaves of bread or skins of wine, that we may test them by tasting. How would you test the truth of a new idea?

Pluto: Well, by examining it from all sides and turning it over and over.

Socrates: But who is to do this? Is there to be a new office created? The Censor of New Ideas, who will examine it and pass it or kill it?

Pluto: No, Socrates. Nothing so ridiculous as that. Let each examine it for himself.

Socrates: And decide for himself?

Pluto: Certainly—or talk it over with others.

Socrates: Well, Pluto, I am afraid that means discussion. Indeed, I know of no way to examine a thought, to see whether it be good or evil, sound or unsound, true or untrue, but to discuss it. So when you say only good thoughts must be discussed, you must admit all thought to be discussed in order to ascertain which are good. Isn't that true?

Pluto: It seems so, Socrates.

Demos: It has certainly been the history of man. What good have we ever achieved save after full discussion, and alas, after bitter opposition?

Socrates: Well, then, if discussion be the way to examine ideas, the fuller, wider and freer the discussion, the better the examination. How does that strike you, Pluto?

Pluto: I see no other answer, Socrates. Unless you limited the discussion to the wise and ruling classes.

Socrates: Who are the wise? The rich?

Pluto: No, not necessarily.

Socrates: The well-dressed?

Pluto: No.

Socrates: The well-born?

Pluto: No, not always.

Demos: "Not always!" Show me the inventors, poets, scientists, artists from the well-born. No, I should say "Not always." Almost never.

Socrates: Well, is there any class of wise men?

Pluto: No, wisdom is not limited to any class.

Socrates: A cobbler might be wiser that a prince?

Pluto: Yes. It is possible.

Socrates: As to cobbling he would surely be more learned?

Pluto: Yes.

Socrates: But if he were ever so wise, and the question to be examined was that of imposing a tax on cobblers, would you let him decide it?

Pluto: No.

Socrates: Or all the cobblers?

Pluto: No.

Socrates: Then if the question to be examined is whether the governing few or the very rich few have unjust Special Privileges, which ought to be taken from them, do you think they ought to be the ones to decide?

Pluto: Perhaps not. But, Socrates, this talk of Special Privileges is all nonsense. These men have had only the same chance that is open to all others. They have earned every cent by their own labors or intelligence, honestly, in a fair field, open to every one.

Socrates: If that be so, then, in my opinion, they ought to be allowed to keep all they have earned, be it much or little.

Demos: I think so, too. But I deny that the field has been free and open, and I deny that they have "earned" their wealth. That is the very subject I want to discuss, and I want to discuss it publicly, and let those opposed speak and let us all hear what is said on both sides.

Pluto: And I say it is outrageous to attack these men.

Demos: I am not attacking any man. I am attacking certain institutions existing in society, which I call Special Privileges, created by force of law.

Pluto: It comes to the same thing in the end. It upsets society, and stops progress. It is nothing less than Socialism.

Socrates: What is that?

Pluto: It is Anarchism.

Socrates: What is that?

Pluto: I am happy to say I don't know, except that they are crazy ideas.

Socrates: But if you don't know what they are, how can you say they are crazy? You must learn, Pluto, not to be frightened at a mere word. Find out what it means before you let it frighten you. But it seems to me, Pluto, you are now denying what before you admitted, and we will never get anywhere unless we settle our points once for all. Do you wish to change your conclusion that new ideas must be discussed to properly examine them?

Pluto: No.

Socrates: And fully discussed?

Pluto: Oh, I suppose so.

Socrates: And not by any class, but by the whole people?

Pluto: No, I don't care to change my ideas on that. It follows, of course.

Socrates: Well, then, let us consider all that settled, and so you see it is not outrageous for Demos here to put out ideas which he thinks right and you think wrong—no matter if those ideas will change conditions in society. Let me ask you, Pluto: Do you think it wrong to seek to change existing conditions?

Pluto: Yes, I do. I don't believe in stirring up discontent.

Socrates: Then you think we are in a perfect condition, and no progress is possible?

Pluto: No, Socrates, you know I don't think anything so foolish.

Socrates: But if it is wrong for us to seek to change conditions, it was wrong for our forefathers to do so, and wrong for their fathers before them, and so on back till we find it was wrong to seek anything better than a cave, a club and some bloody bones. And it will be wrong for our successors to seek to change conditions, and progress must cease, for without change there can be no progress. Is that what you mean?

Pluto: No, Socrates, I don't mean that. But we should be cautious.

Socrates: In other words, we should discuss a long time before we actually experiment. Is that what you mean?

Pluto: Well, I didn't think that was what I meant, but you have a way of putting things so that I am compelled to admit them.

Socrates: Well, don't admit it if it seems false. How would you state it? If we must be cautious we must not make the actual trial till we have thoroughly examined the theory. Is that what you mean?

Pluto: Yes, that is my idea.

Socrates: And to thoroughly examine the idea we must discuss it a long time, thoroughly?

Pluto: Yes. I see I cannot change it from the way you put it.

Socrates: Do you know any other way to finally test a theory but to try it?

Demos: Why do you hesitate, Pluto?

Pluto: Because, if I admit what Socrates first asks me I seem always to be helpless to the end.

Socrates: Surely you would not admit what you could truthfully contradict; let me ask you this: If the known facts are all out of harmony with a theory and contradict it, is the theory true or false?

Pluto: False, Socrates. No doubt of it.

Socrates: Then if you know any way to test a theory other than to put it into practice, and try it out with all the facts, tell me what your way is?

Pluto: No, Socrates, there is no other way.

Socrates: Now, then. I think I understand what you and Demos were quarreling about. It was really whether his notions on Special Privilege and unjust poverty were right or wrong, and you thought they were wrong.

Pluto: Yes, and still think so.

Socrates: Of course, you believe there is right and wrong in the world, Pluto?

Pluto: Oh, yes, that is unfortunately absolutely true.

Socrates: And you adhere to the right?

Pluto: Yes, Socrates, so far as I know it.

Socrates: That is what I mean—you love the ideal Right and hate the ideal Unright, and you will adhere to and battle for Righteousness as you see it.

Pluto: I certainly will.

Socrates: And if by any chance you should be made to see what you thought right was really unrighteous, you would then abandon that and turn always to what you believed to be the right?

Pluto: Yes.

Socrates: So what you really strive for in your soul is not any particular condition, to be maintained by force, be it right or wrong, but to measure that particular thing by the test of ideal righteousness: and if it be wrong, then to abandon it and seek the ideal right?

Pluto: That is how I want to live.

Socrates: Ideal Justice is one form of Righteousness, is it not?

Pluto: The highest form, Socrates. What can be greater than Justice?

Demos: Nothing.

Socrates: Then, Pluto, you believe in justice, rather than Injustice?

Pluto: Most assuredly, Socrates. Who could say he believed in Injustice?

Demos: Oh, nobody says it. But plenty practice it. Words are cheap.

Socrates: Never mind, Demos, Pluto says he will follow Justice wherever he can see it, and will desert Injustice wherever he knows it. Is that right, Pluto?

Pluto: That is right, Socrates.

Socrates: Is it a man's duty to promote justice or obstruct it, Pluto?

Pluto: To promote it, Socrates. No doubt of it.

Socrates: Then the man who believed he saw injustice in an existing system would be wrong in not submitting the question to discussion, which we have seen to be the only test prior to actual practice. Is that so, Pluto?

Pluto: Yes, it seems so.

Socrates: Then I believe, Pluto, you must admit Demos is doing right in discussing those things which he honestly believes to be unjust. And those who so believe, but refrain from agitation and discussion, are cowards or hypocrites. So the only thing left for us to examine is the truth or untruth of Demos's ideas. What is it that he says?

Pluto: He says—

Demos: This is what I say: that the field of struggle is not free and equal to all; that the mother earth, source of all wealth, is given by Special Privilege to a few; that society in general is taxed for a few; that the great economic forces and engines of society are monopolized by a few. And these Special Privileges, like so many conduit pipes, carry the wealth created by the many into the hands of the few beneficiaries of privilege.

Socrates: And what do you say, Pluto?

Pluto: I say it is all nonsense. These same so-called Privileges are open to every man, so therefore they are not Privileges at all. And the wealthy are wealthy because they are superior in industry, intelligence and economy. It is the survival of the fittest, the reward of the most deserving. All cannot get to the top.

Socrates: That is true. But let us examine these questions a little further.

Part 2

April 1911

Demos—Let me say, Socrates, that I consider a Right something which by the common opinion of men is naturally inherent in the individual and in every individual alike, as the right to live and to own those things which he himself has created or purchased with his labor—and a privilege is a special and particular power or enjoyment usurped by the favored individuals, or conferred on them by some one claiming power to do so.

118

Socrates—What have you to say to this, Pluto?

Pluto—I say, as before, Socrates, this thing of rights and privilege is all nonsense. All rights are privileges and all privileges are rights. It is all a matter of the Will of the State.

Socrates—I suppose you will admit that there is such a thing as stealing? Even where there is no society—as one from another, if there were only two persons living.

Pluto—Yes.

Socrates—And if there were only two persons on earth, one might wickedly kill the other?

Pluto—Yes.

Socrates—Are stealing and murder right or wrong in themselves?

Pluto—Wrong.

Socrates—Then if it be wrong to steal another's property the owner must have a right to it?

Pluto—Yes. But, Socrates, you yourself are a witness that a man has not a right even to his life if the State decrees that he must die. So he has not a right to his property if the State decrees that he must give it up.

Demos—You admit though, Pluto, that the State is the only power that has a right to take his life or his property?

Pluto—Certainly. I admit that. And it is the State which gives these rights which you call privileges.

Socrates—The question to be first examined is whether the State has a right to take life or only the power to do so: whether, because the State takes his property from one and gives it to another that makes it right or only compels it and calls it lawful.

Demos—But Socrates, Pluto admits that these privileges rest only in the power of the State, or as he calls it, the consent of society, so I say that the same power which gives them has the power in take them away—and I have the right to persuade society to do so.

Socrates—You speak very practically, Demos, but suppose the State says, as it often does, that you shall not agitate. What then?

Demos—The State cannot suppress thought and speech. It has tried it many times and there are many martyrs to its tyranny, but it cannot do it.

Socrates—But suppose it does? Is that right?

Demos—Well, Socrates, as we agreed some time ago that the whole progress of mankind lay in discovering the truth and that this could only be done by free thought and free discussion, I would think you would see that to suppress thought and speech is not right.

Socrates—In former times they hung men for stealing a few shillings' worth of property. Nay, men were slaves and could be killed at the master's pleasure. Later, though they did not kill them, they bought and sold and used them as cattle. Now, was this right or wrong?

Pluto—Wrong.

Socrates—But the State sanctioned it.

Demos—The State has sanctioned torture and burning alive for opinions' sake and for studying the truths of Nature. The State has given to a few it called lords all the lands—and the people who tilled the land were called serfs—and it has imprisoned and sent to exile or death any who raised voice against this iniquity.

Socrates—Well, I suppose Pluto will admit this is all wrong.

Pluto—Yes, I admit it; but we don't do that any more.

Socrates—I am not so sure. But let us stick to the question. When the State drove men into exile for speaking against injustice or held men in slavery—these things were lawful—were they not, Demos?

Demos—Yes, lawful, for the State; that is to say. The ruling classes make the law as they wish it to be.

Socrates—And the majority of the people accepted these things as right—for example slavery. Did they not, Demos?

Demos—Yes. Most of them accepted it and thought it was right; even most of the slaves thought it was right. The thinkers, the rebels, are always in a minority. But we now have caught up with the rebels and know it was all wrong and it never was right.

Socrates—How do we know it?

Demos—By agitation and discussion which bring us to a better understanding of right and justice: and then by actual practice.

Socrates—Do you mean that man's standard of right and wrong is made by man himself, and what is right at one time is wrong at another?

Demos—Yes, that is what I mean. Of course right and wrong are only relative terms.

Socrates—But we have changed our notions about slavery and about hanging men for petty thefts—and now we know these things were never truly right when measured by the ideal Right and ideal Justice toward which man is groping. How is that, Pluto and Demos?

Pluto—That is true, Socrates. As we now see it, it was never right.

Demos—Of course it was not.

Socrates—Then the State and the majority cannot make wrong right. It can only declare wrong to be "lawful" and compel it by force. Is that so?

Pluto—It seems so.

Socrates—But is it not so? Does might alter wrong into Right, or does might simply compel acquiescence in injustice?

Pluto—Of course it only compels acquiescence, but the people of the time, most of them, acquiesce, because they believe it is right.

Socrates—Compared with Ideal or Eternal Justice, was slavery or wilful slaughter by tyrants ever right?

Pluto—No, it was never ideally right.

Socrates—Might does not make right then, but only makes things lawful or unlawful?

Pluto—Measured by Ideal Right or Eternal Truth, that is correct.

Socrates—Therefore it is not necessarily true that what is lawful is also right—slavery, for instance. What do you say, Pluto?

Pluto—I see no other answer, Socrates. A thing may be lawful and yet prove to be not Right.

Demos—I go further. I say things forced by law are most apt to be unright because decreed by the will of the Ruling Classes for their own benefit. And what a few declare for their own selfish purposes cannot be for the good of the many.

Socrates—Well, it is enough for us to know that Might (or the State) may make the law but cannot change the inherent and eternal wrong into the ideal and eternal right. Lawful and Rightful are not synonymous terms. How does this appear to you, Pluto?

Pluto—It is true: Many unrighteous things have been lawful in their day, I freely admit that, Socrates.

Demos—And the most inherently wicked of all murders is the murder of free thought and free speech.

Socrates—Now then, Pluto and Demos. I think we are prepared to discuss your question, for if I am not in error we have agreed that what is created by law and accepted by society is not necessarily Right, and that it is the duty of all men to discover and follow the Right and that the only road to truth is free thought and free speech—to discover the theory and then actual practice to test the theory. Is this what we have agreed on?

Demos—It is, Socrates.

Pluto—Yes it would appear so, Socrates.

Socrates—You never seem quite sure. Pluto. Even after we have tried every door and found only one which opens to us. Now if you desire to re-argue any point—

Pluto—No. Socrates. That is the last thing in the world which I desire.

Socrates—Pluto, how are we to determine which babies ought to be killed every year?

Pluto—I do not understand you, Socrates. Do you mean which infants will die?

Socrates—No. I mean are there any babies which by the rules of Society are better entitled to live than others? If so, which ones are they and which are the ones to be killed?

Pluto—I still don't understand you, Socrates. Some babies are healthier and stronger than others. Some have better surroundings and a greater hope to live and grow up; but

123

every child has the same right to live; that is to say, in civilized society.

Demos—That shows your ignorance, Pluto.

Socrates—Your remark, Demos, does not help toward the truth. Let us examine this question like philosophers, not politicians. You say, "civilized society," Pluto.

Pluto—I don't know how it might be among savages, Socrates.

Socrates—Well, let us begin with savages, for civilization rests on savagery. Even among savages, or among wild animals, how can you determine at birth or before birth which has better right to live?

Pluto—You cannot do it.

Socrates—Then even among savages the right to live is in all equally, but this right in the weaker may be invaded by the stronger. Just as Society by its strength may invade the rights of the individuals. Is that so?

Demos—You mean all have a right to live if they can, but the stronger will prey upon the weaker so that the weaker will really be exterminated and the stronger will survive.

Socrates—Well, does not that seem so to you?

Pluto—That is correct, Socrates. And I claim in Society it is the fittest who survive.

Socrates—Who are the fittest in Society, Pluto?

Pluto—Those who rise to the top, who lead society, who control things, who succeed.

Socrates—Succeed in what?

Pluto—In their business; in life.

Socrates—Who are looked up to as powerful?

Pluto—Yes.

Socrates—Who dictate the laws and who really rule?

Pluto—Yes.

Socrates—Who have risen above the great common mass so that they really sway the destinies of the masses?

Pluto—Yes.

Socrates—Then those are the ones who best understand and conform to the existing conditions of Society?

Pluto—Yes.

Socrates—The ones who do this in our Society and who are everywhere singled out as the shining marks of success are the great capitalists. They control the lawmakers and the laws. They possess the real power, for they control the capital or accumulated wealth of Society.

Pluto—Certainly they do. It is right.

Socrates—These men are then, in your opinion, more worthy to be crowned by Society than the great leaders of thought, John Brown, Garrison, Lincoln, Emerson, or the great poets, or writers, or teachers, or inventors - is that what you mean?

Pluto—No, I do not mean that. These others have also succeeded.

Socrates—Yes, but not in the conditions of our present Society. They live and die poor. They neither have nor seek power over their fellows. They have no destinies in their hands. As we reckon matters today, which would you say was the successful man—Walt Whitman or J. P. Morgan?

Pluto—Who is Whitman?

Socrates—He is dead. He was a poet who lived in a bare room and died poor.

Pluto—Why, Morgan, of course. I never heard of Whitman. Such a question shows to me, Socrates, that you, too, do not understand our Society.

Socrates—Well, now we know your idea of the fittest to survive in our Society. It is the richest. But tell me, Pluto, which in your opinion is the most desirable on a farm—a flock of hens or a flock of hawks?

Pluto—Socrates, sometimes your questions seem to me absurd. Hens, of course.

Socrates—But often the hawk, which preys on the hens, shows he is the fittest to survive in a struggle where the conditions give a premium to mere powers of prey. I only wanted to get a definition of your words, "In Society it is the fittest who survive." You mean, I suppose, that our present conditions make the man with greatest power to accumulate the fittest to survive. But you will agree that those who may be fittest under some conditions will not be so fit under other conditions. For example, the men who can ride horseback but cannot swim will be the fittest in a cavalry raid and the least fit in a shipwreck?

Pluto—Yes. I admit that.

Socrates—Then when you say the great Industrial Chiefs are the fittest to survive, you mean in Society as it is now ordered?

Pluto—Yes, certainly.

Socrates—So in a savage society the fittest to survive will also be those who kill and take, and we come back to our starting point, that by the laws of Nature each has an equal right to live.

Pluto—Yes.

Socrates—And in this struggle, where each has the same right to keep his own life and all cannot live, each has the right to take the lives of others to keep his own.

Pluto—Yes.

Socrates—And in this struggle the weaker will be sacrificed?

Pluto—Probably.

Socrates—This last and highest right of self-preservation then wipes out all other rights?

Pluto—Yes; certainly.

Socrates—So that if the masses find out that to live they must overthrow the present conditions, and abolish Industrial Chieftains, they have the right of self-preservation to do so?

Pluto—Well, I suppose so if absolutely necessary to their self-preservation. But I deny this—

Socrates—Wait, Pluto. We will take that up later. Let me ask you now, if a stronger savage meets a weaker savage carrying a deer he has killed, and, not needing it that he himself may live, takes it away from him; is that right or wrong, Pluto?

Pluto—Wrong as we look at it, but perhaps not as he looks at it.

Socrates—We are concerned, and must be, with our own conception of the Ideal Right. As we look at it, is it Right or Wrong?

Pluto—Wrong.

Socrates—Why ?

Pluto—Well, because the deer was his.

Socrates—Why?

Pluto—Because he had killed it.

Socrates—Then it was any man's while it ran free?

Pluto—Certainly.

Demos—And became the rightful property of him who secured it by his labor and skill.

Socrates—Suppose the weaker savage discovered a natural meadow of edible roots and while he was digging, the stronger savage came and began to dig also—whose roots are they?

Pluto—They belong to the discoverer.

Demos—I don't think so. He didn't create them.

Pluto—But he found them.

Demos—Someone might have been there before.

Pluto—Then he should have stayed or fenced the meadow or put up a notice.

Demos—The roots existed in Nature and the discovery was an accident. All the discoverer could claim was what roots he could dig.

Pluto—Not at all. The whole meadow was his.

Socrates—For how long?

Pluto—Why, for always.

Socrates —Then he owned all the roots?

Pluto —Certainly.

Socrates —Every year — against everybody?

Pluto —Certainly.

Socrates —He hadn't planted them?

Pluto —No.

Socrates —He hadn't made the soil in which they grew?

Pluto —No.

Socrates —He had merely set eyes on them first?

Pluto —Yes: but for him the meadows might never have been known.

Socrates —Suppose he had discovered a great lake or a sea, would he have a right to all the water and all the fishes?

Pluto —No: but that is different.

Socrates —How?

Pluto —Well, it is water—and larger.

Socrates —Does your rule of right depend on size? Suppose the meadow was exceedingly large?

Pluto —Well, that might make a difference. He might be allotted only a reasonable amount for his use.

Socrates —Who would allot it?

Pluto —The State.

Socrates —Yes, but either one rule is true or the other—either the first discoverer should have all he discovers or he should never have more than his reasonable portion. Now which is right?

Pluto —Well, I think the discoverer should own it because he discovered it, and the State gives it to him as discoverer.

Socrates —If some men who were not born when he discovered at came in his absence and, as they thought, rediscovered it, what then?

Pluto —It would still be his.

Socrates —Really, then, his perpetual ownership depends on his having been born first?

Pluto —Socrates, you make it seem absurd, but nevertheless 1 am of the same opinion I was.

Socrates —As I understand you, Pluto, the man's right to the meadow was because he first saw it?

Pluto —Yes.

Socrates —Then the first man who discovers a new star owns it?

Pluto —No one can own a star, Socrates.

Socrates —Why not?

Pluto —Because you cannot get near it or put it to use.

Socrates —Well, suppose a man sees a deer first and another man kills it. Who owns it?

Pluto —I think, as I said once before, that the man who kills it owns it because the mere seeing it could not prevent the deer from escaping. Killing it gave it into his possession.

Socrates —So if to own a star depends not on seeing it first, but the ability to get it and put it to use, and the ownership of the deer depends on getting possession of it, what have you to say about the roots in the meadow? Does not their ownership depend on getting possession of them and putting them to use?

Pluto — No: I think the man who discovered the field is entitled to all there is in it, especially if the State gives him the title.

Socrates —The State cannot make Wrong Right?

Pluto —No.

Socrates —Suppose the stronger savage must have the roots to keep him alive. We are agreed he may take them?

Pluto —Yes, but only by that necessity.

Socrates —And if the men who were not born when the State gave title to the meadow to the discoverer, need the meadow that they may live, they may rightfully take it, may they not?

Pluto —Oh, I suppose so. But they ought to pay the discoverer.

Socrates —For what?

Pluto —For taking what is his.

Socrates — Ah, yes we must examine that. If the meadow be truly his, they ought to pay him if they can. We will look into that. Let us examine this discovery a little further. If a man on a distant mountain had first seen the meadow and recognized the plant growing in it whose root was desirable, and had started toward it, but the other man had arrived first, though seeing it last, who would have owned it?

Pluto — I think each should be allowed to share in it.

Socrates — Yes, but one saw it first. And you have either a right rule or nothing. Which is it?

Pluto — I will then abide by my rule that he who discovered it.[52] The man on the mountain is entitled to the meadow.

Socrates — Suppose, Pluto, some other men had planted the meadow but for the tops of the plant and knew nothing of the root. Could the man who first discovered the root was good to eat take it away from those who planted it?

Pluto — No; he could not rob those who planted it.

Socrates — But it seems to me to discover that the root was good to eat was a real discovery.

Pluto — That might be a mere accident.

Socrates — Well, what was the discovery of the meadow? But let us drop that for the present. If the stronger man digs some of the roots, in spite of the discoverer, has he taken from him anything he planted or created?

Pluto — No, Socrates.

Socrates — Or anything he ever had of his toil taken into his possession from the hand of Nature?

Pluto — No; but he has taken what the laws of Society would give the discoverer title to.

Socrates — Never mind Society and the laws. We have seen they do not always make a right. We are still dealing with the savages. If the stronger does not take from the weaker what he created or had reduced to his possession, but only side by side with him takes from the breast of Earth—a

---

[52] This somewhat dangling sentence appears in the original.

natural offering to all men, what natural right has he violated?

Pluto — Well, Socrates, it always ends up, as I tell you, I find it difficult to answer you. It doesn't seem to me any natural right has been broken, but we are not savages, and I do feel as if one of our rights of property, as we view it, would have been taken away from the natural owner, the discoverer.

Socrates — Perhaps that is not a right, but one of those privileges which exists not as a just right but only by force of law and the conditions of our society.

Demos — Exactly.

Socrates — Well, let us return to our savages. You admit, Pluto, it would not be right to rob the man of the deer he had killed merely because the robber was a more powerful savage?

Pluto — Yes; it would not be right. I do not think Might makes Ideal Right in one savage any more than in the State. I am certain of that and admit it.

Demos — Pluto, sometimes you are sensible.

Socrates — But if it were a question which of two must die that the other might live, then you think the stronger would prove the fittest to survive?

Pluto — Probably.

Socrates — If the weaker proved more intelligent and scooped from a log a canoe, and wove from fine roots a net and watched for the runways of the fish and caught many of them for himself and his family, and the stronger watched him and robbed him, would this be right?

Pluto — No: it is the same thing—unless he robbed the weaker to save his own life.

Socrates — But if the weaker invented a bow and arrow and slew the stronger, then it would appear as if mere strength were not always the fittest to survive, would it not ?

Pluto — Yes, it would: and that is what I now claim—only the best minds rise to the top.

Socrates — Well, we have been through that as to what are the best minds. We have seen what are best for some conditions are not best for other conditions—and for our present Society it seems they are the minds skilled to acquire capital, or Society's store of wealth; but perhaps if there be a shipwreck it will be found the minds skilled to swim will be better than the cavalry riders. So let us leave the question of who are our most desirable citizens for another solution and stick to this question of Privilege. What would you say if all the tribe got together and agreed that the skilled and cunning fisherman, who labored over his nets and caught many fish, must pay eighty fish out of each hundred to the stronger man, who lay on the rocks and watched the fisherman, doing nothing himself but organizing the tribe so that it would vote him eighty per cent of the fish? Would the vote of the tribe make this robbery of the fisherman of eighty per cent of his toil, any more right ?

Pluto — No, Socrates; it would still be wrong. The tribe could not make right what was not right for the single man to take by force.

Socrates — But if this tribute was voted by the tribe so that all the fishermen of the tribe paid over eighty per cent of the fruits of their labor to ten of the chief men of the tribe, would that alter the Right of the matter?

Pluto — No, we know it would not, Socrates. The man who toils and captures has a right to his capture. It is all his and while force—

Demos — Or say Law—

Pluto — May take it from him, it is not right.

Socrates — What would you call this tribute to the ten chief men from all the fishermen. Pluto?

Pluto — I would call it a tribute or forced tax.

Demos — I call it a Special Privilege given to the ten men—

Pluto — Of course, it is a privilege and is wrong. But I deny that there is any such in our Society. Show me such a privilege and I will join Demos in denouncing it.

Demos — Good for Pluto. Now, then, to show him.

Part 3
May 1911

Socrates: Pluto, when explorers are going through a strange country, it is customary to stop occasionally and note landmarks and set up monuments. Now let us rest here a moment and take account of our progress. We are agreed, are we not, that the state in times past has declared lawful those things which really are and were shameful—such as burning people for their religious opinions and starving thousands that a few lords might have hunting ground. In other words, we are agreed that there is an Ideal Right, and though the state may by its power declare a thing lawful, it cannot make right that which is not right.

Pluto: Yes, we are agreed on that, Socrates.

Socrates: We are agreed that right and wrong are not to be made by law or by that body of persons called the state, any more than by one person, but Right is something self-existent and inherent—and to discover it there must be free discussion and agitation and then practical experiment.

Pluto: Yes, that is true also.

Socrates: And is it true that each is born with the same right to live?

Pluto: Yes.

Socrates: And that self-preservation is the only justification for invading another's right to live?

Pluto: Yes. It is a natural right, equal in all.

Socrates: Then has each the same right to assert it against all others?

Pluto: Certainly he has.

Socrates: Then if it be an actual necessity to save his life, a man may by the law of nature take property or even life—if able to do so?

Pluto: Yes, by the natural law.

Socrates: If that be true of each individual, would it also be true of all individuals collectively?

Pluto: It would seem so, Socrates. I see no reason why any should lose this right in a group.

Socrates: Tell me, Pluto, if you have taken something from me not as the absolute means to sustain your life, but in mere robbery, is it yours or mine?

Pluto: You know, Socrates, what is taken from a man against his will by force or theft is still his, and he may seize it wherever he finds it.

Socrates: Or if I lend a gold goblet to be kept for me—may I have it back when I demand it?

Pluto: Surely, Socrates. Unless you have loaned it to a thief and a villain.

Socrates: Then, if the few have certain advantages which the many need for their own self-preservation, may the many take these advantages from the few?

Pluto: Of course, Socrates, it follows from what we have agreed that if the many need them for self-preservation, they may take from the few just as each one of the many would have a right to take.

Socrates: Now if there should be some privileges entrusted by the many to the few to keep for them, could the many demand them back when wanted?

Pluto: O yes, if there were any such, certainly the right to take them back would exist.

Socrates: Or if the few had robbed the many of any such valuable advantages, could the many undo the robbery and seize them?

Pluto: If what you assume to be true were true, then the many would have a perfect right to retake their own.

Socrates: Then we are agreed that the state may make laws and compel obedience, but cannot make what is wrong Right; that nothing remains fixed, but even our conception of Right and Wrong changes as we press forward toward the ideal; that agitation and discussion as to what is Right or what should be the next step, is not only right in itself, but is the only means of sifting truth from error, and he who refuses to join in the discussion either has no ideas or is a coward—and that if it be found that any have special privileges which are in robbery of others—which any men need to abolish that they themselves may live, these may retake or abolish such special privileges. Are we agreed, Pluto, on all these things?

Pluto: Yes, substantially.

Socrates: Substantially? To what do you not agree?

Pluto: I do not agree that there are such privileges.

Socrates: I know that. I have said. "If it be found that any have special privileges." What do you mean by substantially?

Pluto: Oh, nothing. If you do not expect me to agree that there are special privileges.

Socrates: How would you define a special privilege, Pluto? Give me your idea.

Demos: I—

Socrates: Wait, Demos. Let Pluto speak.

Pluto: Well, Socrates. I hardly know.

Socrates: Would what a man has as a natural inherent right be a privilege?

Pluto: No, that is clear.

Socrates: If a right is a natural inherent right, it inheres in all men equally, does it not ?

Pluto: It would seem so.

Socrates: Then a privilege is an advantage which is not a right? Is that so?

Pluto: Yes. It must be, for if it were a right it could be no privilege.

Socrates: And a special privilege is an advantage enjoyed by a limited or particular class, what would you say to that, Pluto?

Pluto: I agree to that.

Socrates: But a privilege granted to all would put all on an equality and would cease to be a privilege, would it not, Pluto?

Pluto: Certainly.

Socrates: In reality, then, a privilege is an advantage which some enjoy over others.

Pluto: Yes, that is true.

Socrates: Who can grant a privilege?

Pluto: Why, only the supreme authority in the state. I admit the kings of old used to give privileges and monopolies to their favorites, but that time has passed.

Demos: Has it?

Socrates: In our state, who could give privileges?

Pluto: No one can give a privilege but the law-making power.

Demos: Yes, it is always the same. Whoever makes the laws makes the privileges—whether king or congress.

Socrates: So all privileges exist by virtue of law, is that so?

Pluto: Yes, Socrates.

Socrates: Pluto, I have been thinking over that idea of yours, that a man gains a right to a meadow and all the roots in it because he first saw it, and I am not yet satisfied. Is it your idea that he gains a title by discovery to the soil itself or to the roots in the soil?

Pluto: Why, to the soil.

Socrates: But he didn't discover the soil. He doesn't want the soil. He discovered the roots and wants the roots.

Pluto: But the roots are in the soil and make a part of it.

Socrates: How is that?

Pluto: Well, it is the law.

Socrates: O but we are seeking the true right, not the law. The law says much folly. However, suppose the roots had been washed out by a freshet and lay all over the ground, loose—

and he discovered they were good to eat. Would he own the soil on which they lay?

Pluto: Well, Socrates, I don't know. It seems to me if they were not a part of the soil, but dug up as it were, and lying there, then his discovery of them would have nothing to do with the soil. But again, it might be that new crops would come from that soil and they ought to be his.

Socrates: Why?

Pluto: To reward him.

Socrates: For what?

Pluto: For his discovery.

Socrates: We go round in a circle. How about those unborn who are to come after him and desire roots?

Pluto: They must obey the law.

Socrates: The law again. We are seeking the right. Well, let it pass. But if he found the roots lying over the surface of the ground, how many would be his?

Pluto: All of them.

Socrates: And suppose the discoverer had companions?

Pluto: They would share equally.

Socrates: Suppose at the other end of the meadow another man discovered the roots at the same instant?

Pluto: Then he would share also.

Socrates: And if the man who first saw them turned back to tell his tribe about them and meanwhile some one else came and dug up all the roots and carried them off?

Pluto: Well, I suppose in a savage state of society possession would give the roots to the takers, but under our civilized law the man who had title to the meadow could keep all others away.

Socrates: The law again—you should forget it, Pluto. And if this meadow stretched beyond the range of vision—hundreds of miles—would he have title to all of it?

Pluto: No.

Socrates: To how much?

Pluto: I don't know. I suppose the law would give him a liberal quantity for his needs.

Socrates: What have his needs to do with it? If he had a right by discovery he had a right to all, for it is all connected.

Pluto: But he hasn't got any right to it except as given by the laws, and they won't permit him to have more than a reasonable quantity. Otherwise he might own the whole valuable country. He must take what the law allows.

Socrates: If the state allows him half, he has half. If a quarter, a quarter. Is that it?

Pluto: Yes. Whatever the law allows.

Socrates: But suppose others come and say we got here only a few days late. There are enough roots for all. No one planted them. We will take what we need and leave you to take what you need?

Pluto: Then the state would defend the title it has given him.

Socrates: You said the state would only give what he needed?

Pluto: But that is for the state to say. It could give him all if it wanted to.

Socrates: And if it gave him all, it would defend him against those who hungered and would share nature's bounty with him?

Pluto: Yes, it would have to do so, or there would be an end of titles and every one would take whatever he found not taken by others.

Socrates: Now, Pluto, you will admit that all your ideas of what the discoverer ought to have are founded on law?

Pluto: Yes.

Socrates: But you agree that a natural right must of necessity be equal in all men ?

Pluto: Yes.

Socrates: So that all men and every man would have the same equal right to take what lay open in nature, and which no one had actually taken into possession?

Pluto: Yes, of course. If it had never been taken, each and all would have an equal right to take—by the natural right.

Socrates: And the law has altered this natural right?

Pluto: Yes.

Socrates: And who make the laws?

Pluto: The people.

Demos: Ha, ha.

Socrates: Then if the law forbids each to take what he can use, as by natural right he may, and defends one in a large ownership having nothing to do with use or possession, but based on discovery, or title, that discoverer or titleholder has an advantage not common to all and given to him by law. Does that seem so to you, Pluto?

Pluto: But the law gives it to him.

Socrates: We agreed that the law-making power gives all privileges. The question is, does he have a right, equal and common to all? Equal in those who came late: to those who were not born when he discovered the meadow, or does the law protect him against the natural right of others in a peculiar enjoyment of something he did not produce, but which is a part of Nature herself. Which is it?

Pluto: It is the latter.

Socrates: Then by your definition it is a special privilege, is it not?

 Pluto: Yes, in a sense. But others have the same right.

Socrates: Those unborn?

Pluto: They might discover some new lands.

Socrates: It is not difficult to conceive of a time when there would be nothing left to discover, and still the generations of men would crowd on. Suppose it turned out that there were already people living on the land. Who would they belong to?

Pluto: Who, the people?

Socrates: Yes.

Pluto: You know, Socrates, no one could own the people?

Socrates: Who would the land belong to?

Pluto: It would be theirs, as they were there first.

Socrates: But if the discoverer landed at the mouth of a river, how far up the river would his discovery take effect?

Pluto: I don't know. Socrates. A reasonable distance, I suppose.

Socrates: But, Pluto, the law of discovery among nations was and still would be, if there were anything left to discover, that whatever discoverer placed his country's flag at the mouth of a river, his king became the owner of all the land drained by the river and all its tributaries. Thus when De Soto planted the Spanish flag at the mouth of the Mississippi the king of Spain became the owner of all the country to the heads of the Missouri and Mississippi rivers and their tributaries, and the fact that the country was inhabited was of no importance.

Pluto: Yes, but, Socrates, the wild Indians were making no use of the country. They certainly could not keep this country for a hunting ground while Europe needed it to make homes for her starving masses.

Socrates: But the Indians had discovered it first, Pluto, and like your man at the meadow, they were entitled to the whole country.

Pluto: Oh, yes, but it is folly to say a few men have a natural right to keep a great fertile country an unoccupied wilderness. Others have a right to live.

Demos: Good, Pluto. Now you are waking up. The few Indians had no right to the privilege of this country as a hunting ground, and the few capitalistic barons among us have no right to have it kept as their hunting ground, either.

Pluto. There is no comparison. You talk foolishly.

Socrates: Then when the kings wanted to reward a favorite or raise some money, they would give or sell whole areas of their newly discovered dominions and pass it over to the new owner by a piece of parchment. Thus great states were handed over by kings, who never saw them, to men who never saw them. Now tell me, Pluto, what was their right?

Pluto: Well, it was customary. It was the law.

Socrates: Who made the law?

Pluto: The kings did then, in fact.

Socrates: Did the kings make the lands they gave away?

Pluto: No.

Socrates: Tell me how these lands became theirs in true right. Had the kings ever cultivated them?

Pluto: No.

Socrates: Or the men to whom they were given?

Pluto: No.

Socrates: Neither the kings, the grantors nor their grantees had ever seen these lands, yet the title of every acre today depends on those same parchment grants and the right of discovery. Suppose, Pluto, your discoverer had come from the inland toward the sea and had set up his flag on the seashore and had said: "I take possession of every land these tides wash and of all the seas, and all the fishes and pearls in the sea." And then suppose the king had given by a parchment deed grants of lands where there were great cities, and grants of all the pearls and precious corals, and of all the fish in the sea?

Pluto: But, Socrates, that would he the act of a lunatic. No one claims the sea.

Socrates: Why not?

Pluto: Well, it is different.

Socrates: You can map it and mark its boundaries?

Pluto: Yes.

Socrates: Now suppose the king of Spain, or England, or France, gave you a great domain on a piece of parchment and you sailed away to take possession and when you arrived you found it was all sea. What would you do?

Pluto: Nothing, for the sea is not any man's to give.

Socrates: Why is it any less to be given by the king or the State than the vast solitude which no man has seen, yet which the king grants to whomsoever he pleases?

Pluto: Well, Socrates, that is hard to answer, and yet there is a difference between land and sea. I suppose the difference is that you can take possession of the land and hold it and improve it, and this is not possible on the sea.

144

Demos: Good.

Socrates: Wait, Demos. But, Pluto, you can map and plat the sea, survey it and describe it so that the king or State, by the written parchment deed, could grant the sea as well as the land.

Pluto: Well, Socrates, the only reason which I can give is, as I have said, the land is solid, permanent and fixed. A man can go upon it and improve it and change it and put the mark of his labor upon it, so I would say that the distinction is that no man can take possession of the sea, build on it, improve it and make it his abiding-place.

Socrates: Then, Pluto, if we abandon the idea of artificial laws made by kings and states, and seek the very essence of the right to soil, it seems that it really rests on the possession of it and making use of it.

Pluto: Yes, Socrates, it does seem so, though this is a new thought to me and I am not prepared to admit it.

Socrates: Thinking upon the matter the best you can, and placing it upon right rather than arbitrary power or law, what would you say gave the preference of one man over another to any particular part of the earth's surface?

Pluto: I would say getting hold of it first.

Socrates: And what do you mean by getting hold of it? Do you mean a legal title given to him by some power, or do you mean actual possession?

Pluto: I mean the latter, because, Socrates, as we have agreed, all men have an equal right to live, so it would seem to me that all men have an equal right to take possession of that part of the earth which is necessary to their existence, and the man who first does so would have that superior right which comes from actual possession.

Socrates: But this right of possession really depends upon his need, does it not, Pluto?

Pluto: Yes, certainly.

Socrates: Then besides mere possession he must put it to use?

Pluto: Yes, under your theory of natural right this must necessarily be so.

Socrates: And what would be the limit of his possession?

Pluto: As much as he needed for his use, I suppose.

Socrates: It almost seems, then, Pluto, as if the right to the soil depended on the same qualities as the man's right to the deer he had killed. That is, by first securing possession of it and by his skill and labor in making use of it.

Pluto: I must say, Socrates, it does indeed seem so.

Socrates: Pluto, if you found pearls or other fisheries in the sea, the pearls or the fish which you actually caught would belong to you, would they not?

Pluto: Certainly. Those we caught would be ours.

Socrates: Why?

Pluto: Why? Because whose else would they be? We caught them. It was our skill, labor and time, and we would have them in our possession.

Socrates: But any one else could fish alongside of you?

Pluto: Certainly.

Socrates: Then this would not be like the roots in the meadow? This depends also on capture or creation and possession?

Pluto: Yes. It seems so.

Socrates: But the king or state could grant you the sea. Could plat it on a map and could defend you in a monopoly of the pearl fishery, is not that so? It could be done.

Pluto: Yes, it could be done.

Socrates: And if the state did this, would it be a special privilege?

Pluto: Oh, certainly, Socrates. In that case there can be no doubt of it.

Socrates: And if the state grants you a monopoly of a tract of land, by paper title, and defends you in the exclusive title to it so that you may let it be idle while others clamor to use it, as by natural right they could, is that a privilege or not?

Pluto: Socrates, I will frankly admit it is a privilege, just as the monopoly of the sea would be. And I did not, when we began, expect to admit so much; but this privilege is open to every one.

Socrates: Then it is not a privilege. Tell me, Pluto, if a hundred men stand around a greased pole on top of which is a great prize, can they all climb to the top?

Pluto: No, but they can all have a chance.

Socrates: But the first man who climbs to the top will take the prize?

Pluto: Well, they can draw lots for the order of trial.

Socrates: Then the order of trial itself is a privilege. Is it not? And suppose one filled with low cunning rubs himself with rosin dust and so beats his fairer competitors. What have you to say to that?

Pluto: That would be a fraud.

Socrates: But it would win the prize, while the honest herd gaped at the bottom. What do you say, Pluto, to that being the survival of the fittest, and the best man reaching the top?

Pluto: You cannot deny he would be the smartest.

Socrates: And is it your opinion, Pluto, that such smartness is the most desirable thing in human society?

Pluto: No, Socrates I do not really think so.

Socrates: If there was a shipwreck, and only one small raft, floating some distance off, and certain men hurried to swim to it and take possession of it, and others helped the women and children, and when they arrived at the raft, nearly exhausted, those who had first got there beat them off with oars and clubs and forced them to drown. Would you say all had had an equal opportunity?

Pluto: Well, in one sense, they had. Those who aided the helpless, neglected their chance.

Socrates: And is it your opinion then, Pluto, that such persons ought to drown and those who hurried to the raft and took possession are the fittest to survive?

Pluto: No. I don't say that. I think the others finer men—I only speak of the equal chance.

Socrates: If the hare and the tortoise start in a race, have they an equal chance?

Pluto: No.

Socrates: Would you admit that the last swimmers would have a right to get onto the raft if they could?

Pluto: Yes, certainly.

Socrates: And if the first occupants of the raft had more room than was needed for themselves, but from selfishness, still knocked the swimmers over the heads with their oars and clubs, what would you say then?

Pluto: Oh, that would he worse. If there was room for all, certainly those swimming would have a right to force their way onto the raft in spite of the selfish grabbers.

Socrates: And if instead of it being a raft it were a fertile vacant country, what then, Pluto?

Pluto: I see I cannot help giving the same answer, Socrates. Those who needed the vacant land would have a right to take it and put it to use.

Socrates: Suppose, in this struggle for possession of the raft, the captain and crew had taken possession of the boat, and they went among the swimmers and aided the raft-grabbers, as you call them, by helping to knock the swimmers on the head. What would you say as to the equality of the struggle?

Pluto: It would not be an equal struggle, Socrates, certainly.

Socrates: And if the captain and the crew said to those on the raft. "We will see to it that you have a monopoly of the raft and an exclusive use of it and a right to keep it vacant if you please." Would you say that those on the raft were given a privilege or not?

Pluto: Yes, certainly, it would be a special advantage given to them by power or authority and not common to all. So it would be a privilege.

Socrates: Suppose some men were in the hold and could not get out in time to start with the others. Would they have an equal chance?

Pluto: No.

Socrates: An equal chance means equality in all things—time, place, ability, everything involved in the contest. Does it not, Pluto?

Pluto: Yes. An absolutely equal chance means that.

Socrates: Do you think such equality ever exists?

Pluto: No. It is not possible.

Socrates: But if the law takes the place of the captain and crew, and gives to a few, who by reason of being born first,

149

were the first to seize upon the land, the privilege of holding the land, they are favored just as the raft-grabbers were, are they not?

Pluto: Yes, Socrates: I have hesitated to answer these last questions, but I see no escape from it, it would be a privilege. But it still seems to me that others had the same chance to grab the land.

Socrates: Even the babes unborn at the time the land was grabbed? And remember we have seen there is never a precisely equal opportunity.

Pluto: You are always bringing in the "babes unborn." But when they are born and grow up they will have their chances, too.

Demos: They certainly will, and mighty poor ones, unless present conditions are changed.

Socrates: Suppose, Pluto, that you entered a strange country and found, although the land was not all settled upon and in use, yet every foot of it was owned by the king, or a few favorites to whom he had written off a title, giving to this one all the mines or mineral wealth, to another all the timber, to another all the water rights and to another all the fertile acres, and you could not get even a small farm without paying the king or one of his monopolists for it. Would you feel that they had a privilege or not?

Pluto: Yes, Socrates, a very great privilege.

Socrates: And suppose thousands of people came, seeking mines to dig and soil to till and a place for their homes, and they found these natural opportunities lying idle and vacant, would you think that by natural right they could take possession of and use so much as they needed?

Pluto: We have already answered that, Socrates. They would have the right to take for their own use what they found no one else putting to use.

Socrates: And those few who by force of law drove them away or exacted payment from them would have a privilege, would they not, given by law?

Pluto: Yes, Socrates.

Socrates: If you were waiting with a crowd to enter a great treasure-house where were many costly and beautiful things, no two alike, and all of different value, and each person was allowed to carry away some one thing, would you rather enter that treasure-house first or last, Pluto?

Pluto: First, Socrates.

Socrates: Do you know anything made in the stars, Pluto?

Pluto: What do you mean?

Socrates: I mean, did you ever hear of anything made elsewhere than on this earth?

Pluto: No, Socrates.

Socrates: Then all we have comes from the earth, in some way, Pluto?

Pluto: Yes, certainly, Socrates. The earth is our mother.

Socrates: Well, Pluto, I regard the earth as that king's treasure-house and those who get leave by law to hold the valuable parts of the earth vacant till others pay them for its use hold a privilege: those who, like the king, can control the earth, can control their fellows who live upon the earth; and those who can get upon the raft, and hold vacant the places others need to escape from drowning, can dictate the lives of their fellows. And those who have a title which enables them to hold land vacant and idle which others need to use, have a privilege which is opposed to natural right and natural justice, be it in the name of one king or a few who hold under him. Those who first enter the treasure-house will take the most valuable things—the mines, the timber, the water powers, the rich and fertile lands. Those who come after—even the babes unborn—come as servitors in the land of their birth—oppressed by monopolies and special privileges. Now, Pluto, I will be glad to hear what you have to say on this matter.

Pluto: Socrates, I am not one to deny the truth. There may be some answer to what you have said, but I can frame none except that this privilege is of ancient usage and lawful.

Socrates: As every privilege has at some time been—even the privilege of owning slaves. We are agreed, Pluto, are we not, that law cannot make wrong right?

Pluto: Yes, Socrates, to that we are agreed.

Socrates: And are we not also agreed that progress is only another name for change in laws, customs and institutions?

Pluto: Yes, Socrates. We are agreed on that also.

Socrates: Then it seems to me that Demos has a right to agitate for changes which he thinks may abolish these privileges. For if any one is to hush his mouth those holding the privileges will do so, and then there is an end to that free discussion which we have seen is the very life of the search for Truth.

Pluto: So it seems, Socrates. I am a little confused, for this is not the conclusion I expected. Tell me, what other privileges do you assert deprive men of their natural rights.

Socrates: Would you esteem it a privilege if the law allowed some man or set of men to build their castles at the ports or upon the highways and exact toll from all who use the ports or the highways?

Pluto: That would need no discussion, Socrates, it would be a privilege.

Socrates: If a robber, masked and armed, stopped men upon the highway and searched them and took from them what of their possessions he chose, would he acquire a right to the things he stole?

Pluto: No, Socrates. We know he would not.

Socrates: But if the law allowed him to arm himself and rob the travelers or even gave him assistance to take from the travelers, would he then have a right to what he took?

Pluto: Well, Socrates, it seems to me he would have a right, for the general consent of society would have given him, for some reason, the lawful right to take other people's wealth, and that general consent would make his act lawful.

Socrates: Yes, lawful. But law cannot change Wrong into Right. It was not right for him to rob?

Pluto: No.

Socrates: What was his robbery? Was it in taking by force something belonging to another which the other was unwilling to give?

Pluto: Yes.

Socrates: Then if the other is still unwilling to give and the state contributes to the taking from another what is his property and giving it to the robber, it still remains that the property of one is taken from him by force for the benefit of another. Is that so?

Pluto: Yes.

Socrates: And that, we are agreed, is Robbery?

Pluto: No, for the law has made it right.

Socrates: The true Right and Wrong exist of themselves as part of Nature's truth. You agree to that?

Pluto: Yes.

Socrates: So if it is in essence wrong for one man by force to take from another that other's property, the law cannot make that wrong right, but only makes the wrong lawful?

Pluto: It does seem so. Socrates. But when we enter into society we agree to be bound by its laws, and the laws are the will of the majority.

Socrates: Is that so, Pluto? If it be so, it is most interesting. Let us examine it. How did you enter society?

Pluto: Why, I was born in this country.

Socrates: And when you were born did you sign a contract to be bound by the will of the majority?

Pluto: No, but it has to be so.

Socrates: Who says so?

Pluto: Well, society—the laws.

Socrates: So the laws speak for the laws, and say all must obey them?

Pluto: Certainly.

Socrates: Then as most people are born into the society in which they live, there is no agreement at all, but only the compulsion of the law?

Pluto: But if most people objected to the law they would change it.

Socrates: That, too, is interesting. Do you think most people in Russia approve the tyrannies of that oligarchy?

Pluto: No.

Socrates: Did most people approve the tyrannies of such monarchs as Nero?

Pluto: No.

Socrates: Do most people approve today of the High Protective Tariff, or the election of United States Senators by the legislatures?

Pluto: No, I do not think they do.

Socrates: Then laws are not always the will of the majority.

Pluto: No, not always.

Socrates: We are agreed that a Privilege is a special favor to a few?

Pluto: Yes, Socrates.

Socrates: And these favors are created by law?

Pluto: Yes.

Socrates: And created directly or indirectly by those interested?

Pluto: Yes, that is true, Socrates.

Socrates: Then in fact these Special Privileges are the creations of the few interested ones and are accepted dumbly by the many. Is not that the truth of history, Pluto?

Pluto: I fear it is, Socrates.

Socrates: So that the man who is privileged to rob does not even have the will of the majority, but has the will of himself and associates not resisted by those who are unwillingly robbed. Do you remember, Pluto, that you agreed it was wrong for a few to lie on the rocks and watch the industrious fishermen catch fish and then persuade the tribe to force the fishermen to give to the idlers on the rocks a part of their hard-earned catch?

Pluto: Yes. I have no desire to change my opinion on that.

Socrates: Then if you are born into a society which permits a few to take a part of your earned wealth from you under penalty that if you refuse you will be sent to jail or punished—how do you distinguish that in essence from the robbery of the fishermen or by the lone highwayman?

Demos: The highwayman is a better fellow. He is bolder and would respect the poor.

Socrates: Wait, Demos. Now, Pluto, you, by your name, ought to know what money is. What is it?

Pluto: It is something we exchange for commodities we want.

Socrates: If there were no money of any sort, men would have to barter among themselves. Exchanging goods till each got what he wanted?

Pluto: Yes.

Socrates: And the best that could be done would be to have local markets or exchanges, where people could meet to swap their properties around?

Pluto: Yes.

Socrates: If there were no money, free exchange of commodities by means of money as a measure of value and medium of exchange, would be impossible? There would be no commerce?

Pluto: Yes, that is true.

Socrates: So money is as important as ships or cars, in commerce?

Pluto: Yes, Socrates.

Socrates: And there are several kinds of money—money of intrinsic value, which is as valuable melted as when stamped by the state: for example, gold. And credit money, such as notes, sometimes secured by special properties, as government bonds.

Pluto: Yes, Socrates.

Socrates: Now, Pluto, you will easily agree that the value of this article called money depends on the relation of the demand to the supply precisely as does the value of wheat?

Pluto: Yes, Socrates. Essentially so.

Socrates: Then if any set of men can control the money supply, is that a privilege just as if they controlled all the ships, or cars, or the wheat?

Pluto: Yes, Socrates. It is a great privilege and power.

Socrates: This credit money depends on the credit of those putting it out and the securities on which it rests, does it not, Pluto?

Pluto: Certainly.

Socrates: Then if one certain class of securities, very limited in number, is by force made the sole foundation for circulating notes, those men who get that security in their control will control the money of the country, will they not?

Pluto: Yes, Socrates, that must inevitably follow.

Socrates: Is this a privilege, Pluto?

Pluto: Socrates, I can only answer that it is. A most valuable one. But it seems to me all have an equal chance to get that security, do they not?

Socrates: How about the babes unborn?

Pluto: There you go again, Socrates, about the babes unborn.

Socrates: But, Pluto, you must see that any institution which forestalls the natural and equal right of the unborn generations is an unjust institution. Because the equal right to live and seek happiness is always equal save as altered by the laws of Nature. You have admitted this. Do you desire to re-examine the question?

Pluto: No, Socrates, because as I have said before, if I answer your questions as it seems to me they must be answered, you always bring me to your conclusion.

Socrates: That is nothing, Pluto, and of no value unless your mind is convinced. If you can find better answers or better questions you ought to do so. But let us drop the babes unborn if they irritate you, and let us return to our raft. If the state makes a small raft and says to all the swimmers, the first who get control of this raft shall hold all the less fortunate in perpetual control, would that be right?

Pluto: No, Socrates, I must answer that it would not.

Socrates: Is it more right for the state to make a limited raft on which to float its money, which is called the life blood of commerce, and give control of it to a few men and compel all others to come to them and buy money from them?

Pluto: Buy money, Socrates! What do you mean?

Socrates: You surely have heard of interest, Pluto?

Pluto: Yes, certainly.

Socrates: Well, interest is the price of money, and were men free to issue credit money as demanded on other good securities than government bonds, money would come into use as needed, and interest would always be very low. This is called Free Banking. Have you never heard of this, Pluto?

Pluto: No, I never have.

Demos: That is because you are a banker.

Pluto: But this would lead to unsafe, reckless issuance of money.

Socrates: Why?

Pluto: Well, I think it would.

Socrates: The men who bought money would want good safe money, would they not?

Pluto: Oh, they would, if they could know it.

Socrates: Well, who would know?

Pluto: Why, only the bankers—the experts.

Socrates: But some bankers were grocers or lawyers before they were bankers. Do they have a peculiar intelligence as bankers?

Pluto: No, but I think they ought to control the money.

Socrates: Well, you would agree then that they are the best judges as to what securities to issue money on?

Pluto: Yes, I agree to that.

Socrates: But if all the bankers met in convention and decided on what securities to issue money? They can now only issue on government bonds. That is the law.

Pluto: Well, that does not seem right.

Socrates: No. The bankers do not think it is right when they desire to violate it, because when they wish to issue additional money in times of urgent demand they do so and call the money "Clearing-house Certificates."

Pluto: Yes. I know about them, Socrates. And you must admit they brought great relief, and justified the temporary breach of the law.

Socrates: I do admit it, Pluto. So much so that they proved the law ought to be broken forever. What is useful and true at one time is useful and true at all times.

Pluto: I am afraid, Socrates, that I am compelled to admit that this right to issue bank notes on government bonds alone is a great and powerful privilege.

Socrates: And those who control the bonds control the money issue, and its limited quantity makes it high priced, or in other words, interest is high?

Pluto: Yes, Socrates.

Socrates: Well, Pluto, this is enough. You have admitted that there are privileges and that the right to discuss them is not only a right, but a duty, so do not find fault any more with Demos.

Demos: Socrates, you asked Pluto if a man or a few men had a right to rob the passers-by on the highway, and he said they had no such right, and then as I understand it he also admitted that while the state might make lawful this blackmail and aid in collecting it, yet it was no more right than before. He has also admitted that what a man creates or earns is his own. I would like to ask Pluto if a man has a right to spend the wealth he has earned so as to give him the greatest benefit?

Pluto: As I understand the question, I would say he has a right to do with his own as he pleases.

Demos: Would it be right for the state to compel a man who can get two pigs for five dollars from a neighbor, to take only one pig—no better—from another man and pay five dollars for it?

Pluto: Demos, you ask foolish questions. Let Socrates ask the questions.

Socrates: Oh, Demos is doing well. We are apt to think questions foolish when we do not understand.

Demos: In plain language is it morally right, or, right by nature, for the state to compel its citizens to pay higher prices for all commodities made within a certain line, when men just over that line will sell better goods cheaper?

Pluto: No, that is not right in essence.

Demos: It is not so bold nor any more right than the highwayman's robbery.

Pluto: But no state does this. No people would submit to it.

Socrates: Perhaps not, for you say the people make their own laws. Demos is speaking of the Protective Tariff. Pluto, it is a forced tax, taken from the consumers' pocket to give to a few manufacturers. Are they privileged or not?

Pluto: Yes, of course, they are privileged, but the chance is open to all.

Socrates: Can all be manufacturers? Can all get on the raft? No. Pluto, the great privileges are the privileges to monopolize land; to monopolize money, and the taxing power, which takes from the many by force of law and power of the state a portion of their hard earned wealth to give as bonuses or subsidies or tariff rates to the privileged few.

Pluto: Socrates, I am not equal to debate with you and Demos. Much of this is new to me. But how would you change things for the better?

Socrates: Freedom. The remedy which man has found in all his history for his artificial oppressions. Free Trade. Free Ranking. A Free Earth, the same title to land as to the fish and the deer. The title by subduing it, possessing it, putting it to a beneficial use. The same title by which men hold water for irrigation, mining or other purposes. No man is permitted to own more than he can beneficially use. And let me ask you, Pluto, for you are a young man: Do you respect the highway robber? The man who preys upon others? Who takes by force what he has not earned?

Pluto: How could I respect such a one?[53]

Socrates: The time will come, Pluto, when those who take as now by force of law, taking by shrewdness and covert force for themselves that which others have earned by the sweat of their faces, will be regarded not as the best citizens of society, but as we now regard robbers. It needs only the awakening of the minds of men to the truth, those who now see no wrong in their unearned wealth will be ashamed of it, as the pirate might be, for he, too, is a leader among men. The best citizens will be those who lead men nearest to Truth, and through Truth unto Freedom and Happiness.

---

[53] The original read "such an one."

Selections from *Too Much Government* (1931)

Wood's *Too Much Government* is probably his least successful book, in the sense of a complete work. The reason for this is that half of it is about minor details in the fight over Prohibition, and even those sections that were once timely are overcooked and far too long. There are also a number of sections about Russia that are of some historic interest but which are not particularly connected to the theme of libertarianism.

That said, some sections of the book represent perhaps the clearest, most distilled statements of Wood's political and social philosophy. Therefore certain quotes that are particularly well-written and at least somewhat connected to the theme have been extracted to print here.

Wood used few paragraph breaks; some of the longer ones have had breaks added to make them more readable. The page number follows each quote. In a few cases an explanatory note [*in bracketed italics*] has been added.[54]

---

[54] Photo, Oregon Historical Society Research Library no. ba018079

✦

Of all the stupid solemnities of courts I think the stupidest is, "Liberty cannot be permitted to pass into License." If any power can say what is Liberty and what is License, then there is no Liberty. Liberty means the right to peaceably say all things and peaceably do all things; being answerable for the consequences. *16*

✦

Given a government with power over property and power to grant privileges, and as surely as water cascades down the mountain, you will find that government will be owned by those having privileges and desiring more. *38*

✦

My own theory is not communism. I am an extreme individualist, but I am so against the feudal system that I am ardent for any change. I would support any of the schools for new social order. They all have one principle in common—to do away with the feudal system of special privileges, inequality and injustice. *57*

✦

I would like to see these men of power animated by that profoundest unselfishness which is the noblest selfishness — do as you would be done by—that unselfish selfishness which makes the honey bee eager to die in the service of the hive. I know that when this day comes these captains will be more zealous and delighted in the higher calling than ever they were living only for self and a privileged few at the expense of the people, at the expense of the future, at the expense of the race. If I could work a miracle I would have our captains see that this moving mass we call the people with all its ignorance, stupidity, vice and squalor is the human race. In it is the far future, the dreamland of Man's intellect, the bright and blinding altar of his soul. All is there. All wisdom, all vision, imagination, joy, hope and beauty of a world to be.

I would have each say to his own heart, just as eagerly as he now whispers "More money," "More power," "I will be one of the Immortals to heal poverty, to abolish injustice and to lift up this mass to a higher level, and higher and still higher, up through many levels, each of more happiness, more beauty, more worth of soul, till this little globe and the cosmos shall inherit from Man such justice, genius, beauty, happiness, as perhaps God himself has never dreamed." Captains, overlords, millionaires, would not this be nobler than gifts, charities, foundations from unearned or ill-earned wealth, leaving the source of human misery to flow?—greater than any triumph in industry or finance the slave-making system invites you to? *89*

✦

[on nudity]
There are, I believe, more than four hundred stripes and shades of Protestants. How they dipped their various quarrels out of the small pool of the Gospels I do not understand.

165

That is their business. It shows great ingenuity and an earnest Christian endeavor to send souls to hell. The only real authority we have says that God made man in his own image, and let it go at that. He himself does not ever seem to have been ashamed of His image or His handiwork. But it seems to be an obsession of some of his special attorneys that he is now acutely shocked and wants his great mistake covered up. Possibly, in the beginning, he had no mirror. 96

✦

[on the question of whether Edouard Bourdet's play The Captive *and Radclyffe Hall's novel* The Well of Loneliness, *which deal with homosexual desire, are obscene]*
Play and book deal in a lofty sympathetic way with an affliction which even scientists are only beginning to understand—homosexuality. But homosexuality is life, and a tragedy of life. If the madness of Ajax or Orlando or Hamlet are fit studies for art in tragedy, so is this complex inheritance inflicted on the child in its mother's womb.

In her laboratory, Mother Nature uses two principles for the continuation of life—the male and the female. Sometimes, as in some plants and lower forms of animal life, both sex principles are in the same individual. But in her experiments in evolution into higher forms of life this Mother of ours as a rule quite distinctly separates the male and female into different forms, and gives to each a particularly physical attraction for the opposite sex. But when our Mother comes to the problem of an advanced type—Man—with a whole battery of glands, nerves, and subtle emotions to deal with, the laboratory intricacy becomes too complicated for our simple Mother, accustomed as she is to turning out just "male" or "female" physically and calling it done; her hand shakes or she forgets something; and the girl will fall in love with a girl and the boy with a boy—fall in love emotionally, but by no means always physically. In other words, the freak girl is cursed with a masculine emotionalism toward girls, and the man-abnormality is attracted to men.

It is a great curse, as is any abnormality. How great a curse—how difficult and hopeless a situation—only the scientists and the victims know. It is a blunder of Nature that calls for all the pity we are capable of. Every reasonably well-informed person now knows that this abnormality is not obscene, but is a most pathetic phase of human life, quite common; and its study and its tragedy are as much the fit subject of art as they are of science. To read about it or see a drama founded on it will no more corrupt the young than to see *Macbeth* or *Hamlet*. The subject is a study in human psychology and suffering, as jealousy is, or any other mania; and to see such a play or read such a book can no more make a person a homosexualist than it can make a man a woman, or a woman a man. The "making" is done before birth; in the laboratory of our bungling old Mother.

To real human beings who know anything, the suggestion is not obscenity but a tragic pathos. But of course our densely ignorant "vice" hunters who get their morals from some mental sewer, and the mob that trails after them up to the judicial bench and shows the ignorant judge how much ignorance he can count on at the next election, are neither human nor informed. This play and this book which I have selected from among many suppressed in this very ignorant, insular republic, were respectively produced and published in France and England, and hailed by press and people as works of art and as missionary tracts in the labyrinth of human psychology.

But why need Watchers and Warders and Vice Suppressors seek knowledge from God's later revelations to Science? Are they not God's policemen to keep the earth rotten in spite of his own efforts to keep it pure? The real motivating foot that steps on the gas is their own ego. They burn to make the world over, not in God's image, but in their own. They wouldn't know the Prince of Peace and Preacher of Tolerance if they met him. They can easily find him if they truly want him. *110-111*

✦

Art cannot work by innuendo. It must work as the sun works—serenely, in the open, or not at all. So Art suffers at the obscene hands of those not fit to tie her shoe latchets. If it be art, there can be no more obscenity in it than there is in a naked baby flirting with a sunbeam. Art is never obscene—as sunrise, birth, love, and death are not. The point is, where did "Government"—ignorant government, ignorant men, puritans and politicians—get this fearful power to interfere? *113*

✦

The Better American Federation,[55] having no experience with ideas, suppresses everyone found carrying an idea concealed about him without a permit. *127*

What I am obstinately hoping for is evolution in freedom and in peace, not a revolution in blood. Will you allow it? It is not possible without free speech. Dear young people, bubbling over with what you call patriotism, stop a minute! Think hard. Where would we be today, where would the world be, if someone, sometime, somewhere, had *not* opposed "organized" government? If you didn't learn it in school, begin a night school with yourself and learn now that everything that makes life worth living, everything that makes man's soul and body his own, everything that differs freedom from crushing despotism has been wrung from "organized governments" by disobedience to the law. If you want your children to be happy, if you want history to write of the United States as anything else than one more imperial despotism of over-piled wealth on the backs of the oppressed and poverty-wrung common mass, you had better stop talking of "organized government" and "obedience to law." Remember there is something greater than law. That is freedom, and the natural inherent rights of man. *131*

---

[55] This passage contained a somewhat humorous typo (presumably, though Wood's sense of humor was unpredictable), making it the "Butter American Federation," in the original.

One moonlight night we were riding up the Malheur Canyon—sometimes stirrup to stirrup, sometimes Indian file. Out of the dark depth of the canyon, the rushing Malheur River tossed up to us the jewels of the moon. We fell to philosophizing, as one does under the influence of the moon—a sort of moon-madness released in the quiet of the night—and old Billy told me of his start in life: "A lean little boy ... I was brought up by an awful good man. He was religious, too awfully religious, and when I was leaving, he says to me, says he, something I ain't never forgot—never. Says he, 'Billy, always remember the other fellow, by God!' No, he didn't say that—he was awfully religious. Says he 'Billy, always remember, by Jesus Christ, the other fellow may be right!'"[56]

The moon understood, the great lava cliffs understood. It was true—true as the great black walls that once were fire. *"The other man may be right."* It should be posted in every police station, in every office of power and authority, in the churches and cathedrals where Jesus Christ is a long-dead name. *138*

✦

The makers of this republic and its constitution knew the evils of government. They feared the steady growth of power and tyranny with the growth of riches, centering in a privileged class. They dreaded a centralized government of dominant power—that would be a power more easily

---

[56] The likely origin of Wood's inscription to his son noted on p. 18.

controlled by a ruling class—and they put their faith in local self-government, as the only guarantee of freedom. Each community was to be the judge of its own affairs. So they were very jealous for the powers of the independent states, and very fearful of the power of the federal Government. They felt the purpose of the general government was only to do those international and interstate things none of the states could or ought to do; those things which related to the whole confederation and as to which no one state or group ought to be the governor, with the bitter experience that government is an evil and not to be trusted, the several states limited the government of the United States by a written charter, in and by which they united in giving to the Federal Union what powers they delegated to it and no other, all other powers being reserved to the several states.[57] This charter they called a Constitution—and besides the limited powers carefully named given to the general government, they put into the Constitution, as I have said, a provision that all powers not given to the Federal Government were reserved to the several states. *143*

In short, the whole effort of the Founders was to limit and hold down the power of the United States (the government at Washington), and to preserve to the fullest extent the sovereign power of the independent states except as expressly

---

[57] One of the curiosities of this section of Wood's commentary is that he, one of the great 20th Century champions of the individual, should so state the content of the 10th Amendment, which actually reads "The powers not delegated to the United States by the Constitution, nor prohibited by it to the States, are reserved to the States respectively, *or to the people.*" Emphasis added. It may be that for him the states and the people were one, at the time, or by comparison to the federal government.

limited in favor of the general government by the Constitution. *143-144*

But so enormous has been the force of gravity of privileged wealth—its interests being best served by a central government—that whereas the effort of the founders was to limit and shackle the general government as much as possible, the stupid effort of their successors has been not only to acquiesce in every encroachment on local self-government by "Uncle Sam" but to have the people of the states eagerly shovel on to the government at Washington everything the states are too shortsighted, too poor, or too indifferent to do for themselves. The popular slogan has become "Let 'Sam' do it." As "Sam" has a constantly hungry political family about him, eager for more and more offices, the functions of "Sam" and the offices at his disposal have continually multiplied. Now he has the power and equipment of a great empire. A good primer for the eighth grade would be a simple list of "Sam's" activities, the number of his servants, the buildings required for them, and the cost of keeping them and their functions. ... *144*

✦

"State-rights" got a bad name when before and during the Civil War it became synonymous with Slavery; and the common people never will, probably, gain any idea of its true meaning. "State-rights" is really local self-government. Local self-government is called the cornerstone of Anglo-Saxon Liberty. There is not enough liberty anywhere to brag about.

But what there is, English, French or Chinese, does rest on local self-government—the right of the smaller self-contained groups to govern themselves. Our groups by origin and custom are the States. Every time a State lets "Sam" at Washington meddle with its own local affairs, it makes a mistake and loses freedom—and pays a price.

Local self-government, or State-rights, really means freedom—that relative freedom of every peaceable man to live his own life his own way, preserving the same right to others. This individual freedom enlarges to the right of each self-contained community to live its own peaceable life in its own way, preserving the same right to other communities. *144-145*

✦

Torquemada and the Holy Office professed a wish to save the world from heresy; in fact, as with all prohibitionists what really animated Torquemada and the Inquisitors, and what now moves our drink tyrants and crusaders, was and is an enormous egotism. They and they alone are right, and their egotism is a fierce determination to compel all others to *their* will. No one can by force and compulsion take care of another's soul. *165*

✦

Perhaps I am a fanatic for freedom, but I would leave every peaceable person absolutely free and unmolested in his own ideas—his own living. These are his very soul, where neither I nor another has a right to meddle. If I thought him wrong I

173

would try to reform him, and so reform society, by discussion, persuasion, reason. I would try to reach the mind with ideas not the body with slugs from a sawed-off shotgun. I have looked back somewhat, even to the time of Lao-tze, and I have found nothing educative or convincing in force, nothing valuable in force except as a protective defense against force. *186*

✦

Why man's soul cannot be viewed as the real instrument for progress and left absolutely free in its peaceable orbit, I cannot comprehend. Why the earth cannot be viewed as one friendly garden exchanging merchandise and good will with each other, I cannot understand. In this I admit I am a fanatic. But I like to think that in this, Jesus and all the wise are with me. *187*

✦

Who has succeeded in moral reform by force? Name one. And be not deceived. The freedom to eat as I like, drink as I like, read as I like, play as I like, are all one with the freedom to think as I like, speak as I like, or pray as I like. Whatever the courts of power and force do not like, they call abuse of freedom, but the distinction is simple and clear: everyone should be free in *all* things so long as he is peaceable and allows the same freedom to others; when he becomes riotous and dangerous by acts that threaten the peace and safety of others, that is abuse, and should be dealt with as any other abnormal, forcible threat to society... . *211*

✦

If the church that says it enters politics and violates my freedom for the good of others, I answer; that has been the everlasting cause of hell upon earth–that is in Torquemada's vein; I answer, when "others" are breaking glass and the peace, attend to them, but let decent, peaceable me alone.   If you desire to reform, do it by education and persuasion. Good is not accomplished by compulsion.   Least of all is it accomplished by compulsion of the self-controlled for a supposed benefit to the uncontrolled.

Intemperance in drinking is not cured by intemperance in sawed-off shotguns.   Indeed, intemperance in governing another's life is worse than drunkenness. No man is good enough or wise enough to govern another in his own affairs. To change habits, to reform morals, is not a police matter, but as the wise Lincoln said, it is matter for education and persuasion. Those calm observers who look at us from a safe distance, overseas, say that we are a "nation of preachers," that we are "emotional, not reasonable," and that our emotions are only "two jumps from insanity." That when we discover an evil, our "first thought is to pass a law against it" and "the next step is to break the law." We continue, however, to think the remedy for everything from Limburger cheese to prostitution is a law. *219*

✦

Remember this, dear reader, gentle reader, dear citizen, gentle citizeness. When you outlaw a thing you not only put it beyond the protection of the law, but you put it beyond *control* of the law. *250*

✦

One who reads this slight book will understand as I do that it by no means exhausts the subject of "Too Much Government"—either in facts or in spirit. It scarcely touches it. We are interfered with and accustomed to control and dictation from the cradle to the grave in thought, speech and act, in work and play, in morals and manners, in habits and costumes. If in anything we seem free, it is only because our despot is indifferent and has not yet chosen to dictate. Always there was that much freedom to the most servile peoples. The soul of freedom, the understanding of what is the true sphere of government, the aroused defiance against all tyranny, the resentful, angry resistance of free men to every invasion of their god-given rights, is dead.

We are thoroughly prepared to be submissive slaves in a great imperialism, and so long as we ourselves are not smitten we care not that another's freedom is being slain. We do not fight that others may have freedom in the opinions we hate. We reverence the policeman's club because it is "Law"— when in fact it is generally only the policeman's will, conscious of the brutal power of the state back of him; and every instinct should teach us that most law is oligarchic *despotism,* and no law is entitled to blind obedience.

I am fully aware that this book will have no more effect than a raindrop in the Atlantic. Freedom is not made by books, and a free people does not need books to teach it freedom. But I have written for those few who, not needing any teaching, yet will, I hope, get that sort of comfort a little knot of sheep feels, huddled in the lee of a cliff, and feeling they are not utterly alone. And perhaps it may hand on a torch in a dark night. *Conclusion p 266*

Index

Photo credits

Sara Bard Field Ehrgott with Wood, Oregon Historical Society Research Library photo, bb002909.

Front cover inset: C.E.S. Wood, Sep. 13, 1937.
(Photo by Dr. William K. Livingston, "Charles Erskine Scott Wood," *Lewis & Clark Digital Collections*, accessed September 25, 2014, http://digitalcollections.lclark.edu/items/show/5901.)

Cover: Fish Creek Basin, Steens Mountain, Oregon. Photo by Alan Contreras.

About the author

 **Alan L. Contreras** is a writer and higher education consultant. His previous books include *College and State, Afield: Forty Years of Birding the American West, Song After All: The Letters of Reginald Shepherd and Alan Contreras* and others. He is a distant relative of well-known libertarian writer Rose Wilder Lane (1886-1968). He is a fourth-generation Oregonian and a graduate of the University of Oregon and its law school. He lives in Eugene, Oregon.